T0193619

THE ABCS OF BIBLE HEROES AND HEROINES

Peggy Shaw

WESTBOW
PRESS®

A DIVISION OF THOMAS NELSON
& ZONDERVAN

Scripture quotations from THE MESSAGE. Copyright © by Eugene H. Peterson 1993, 1994, 1995, 1996, 2000, 2001, 2002. Used by permission of NavPress. All rights reserved. Represented by Tyndale House Publishers, Inc.

Scripture quotation taken from the King James Version.

WestBow Press books may be ordered through booksellers or by contacting:

WestBow Press
A Division of Thomas Nelson & Zondervan
1663 Liberty Drive
Bloomington, IN 47403
www.westbowpress.com
1 (866) 928-1240

ISBN: 978-1-9736-1751-8 (sc)
ISBN: 978-1-9736-1750-1 (hc)
ISBN: 978-1-9736-1752-5 (e)

Library of Congress Control Number: 2018901185

Print information available on the last page.

WestBow Press rev. date: 02/16/2018

Dedication

This book is dedicated to my five precious grandchildren: Shaw, Jenkins, and Tommy Legare, Abbey and John Hiott. Nana's prayer is that my grandkids will read and study and exemplify the lives of the heroes and heroines of the Bible. I want them to know that God has used, in the past and still does, ordinary people to do extraordinary things because our God is so powerful and so mighty. Hebrews 4:12 says, "For the word of God is quick and powerful and sharper than any two-edged sword piercing even to the division of the soul and spirit and of the joints and marrow, and is a discerner of the thoughts and intents of the heart." KJV

Foreword by Michael W. Bearden
Retired Senior Minister of First Baptist Church,
Fountain Inn, South Carolina

The Bible says, "Train up a child in the way he should go and when he is old he will not depart from it." (Proverbs 22:6) And there is no better way to train children than to teach them the stories of the great people of the Bible who trusted and lived for God. Peggy Shaw has done a wonderful service in condensing the stories of the characters of the Bible with their corresponding lessons in The ABCs of Bible Heroes and Heroines. She gives the reader a glimpse of the great characters of the Bible along with their struggles as well as victories in Jesus. She highlights a major lesson or two from their lives that children of all ages can understand. In this day when children are being so negatively influenced from all directions I would highly recommend that parents and others who work with children and are interested in teaching them godly values, use Peggy's work as a primer alongside their Bible in leading children to develop the right kind of values that will carry them through life.

Foreword by Dr. Condy Richardson

Lead Pastor of First Baptist Church, Fountain Inn, South Carolina

We all have a story. Every family has adventures, disappointments, secrets ... and stories. The Bible is the Christian's family storybook. In these holy words, we learn of godly Father Abraham and mischievous Jacob. We also learn that we should never judge a book by its cover. What a fantastic family storybook! Peggy Shaw knows children. She has given her adult life to educating, molding, and mentoring young boys and girls at Fountain Inn Elementary School and Fountain Inn Baptist Church. She is immensely talented and energetic, and Peggy has done her research. These Bible stories are part of her DNA, and she still marvels at them. Peggy has scoured the Bible and has a keen grasp of the detail and background of the lives of these colorful characters. These narratives and characters move her and shape her life. May they change your life as well. Enjoy this book! In The ABCs of Bible Heroes and Heroines, Peggy presents biblical prose in readable portions so a child can remember what he or she has read. Her writing is clear and concise. The stories are timeless. As you read these wild, bizarre, and heavenly stories, remember that they are just the tip of the iceberg. In John 21:25 John says the world is not big enough to hold all of the stories of Jesus in book form. You are part of his story as well. The story of God goes on. As you read The ABCs of Bible Heroes and Heroines let Jesus show you inspire you what is next in your story. Happy reading!

Aaron was a half brother to Moses,
and he was three years older.
God sent them both to Egypt to see its leader,
Pharaoh.
Moses was to do God's miracles.
Aaron was to say, "Let My people go."
God used both brothers even through one was shy;
the other one was bolder.
Later, Aaron became a priest to the Israelites.
He was their spiritual leader.
Moses met with God to receive the Ten
Commandments on Mt. Sinai.
Aaron melted all the people's rings and necklaces
and formed a golden calf.
The people could bow down and worship it,
and even offer sacrifices
to this man-made god.
When Moses asked Aaron to explain how the idol
was made and why,
Aaron said the gold was just thrown into the fire,
and out came this creature with two ears.
This idol worship caused Aaron and the Israelites
to wander around aimlessly in this desert sand
for another forty years.

Abel was the second child born on Earth.
He was the younger brother of Cain by birth.
Their parents were Adam and Eve.
Together, they were the first family.
The brothers grew up watching Adam offering
a sacrifice once a year
to God to receive His blessings
and forgiveness of their sins.
When old enough to make their own sacrifices,
each had an important choice to make
as the time drew near.
Each boy wondered what gift was good enough
to offer Him.
Abel offered a perfect little lamb—his very best.
The lamb's blood was shed.
Able had obeyed God's law.
God was pleased with Abel's gift.
However, Cain gave some fruit to God.
Cain badly failed the test.
Cain became jealous of Abel.
This was more than just a little rift.
Unfortunately, the anger grew until Cain
killed Abel, his very own brother.
What a shame! This sinful action
was Earth's first murder.
Any sin seed can grow and flourish
out of control,
and can multiply to spread out
over the container's rim.
So give God the very best you have.
God wants your obedience more than
any sacrifice that you could possibly
offer to Him.

Abigail was the beautiful wife of Nabal.
Once David sent ten men to visit Nabal.

Nabal acted very rudely.
When David found out about Nabal's behavior
toward his men,
he became so angry that
his army he did send
to show his bitterness at this action
and to raid Nabal's property.
As a wife should try to protect her husband,
Abigail did her duty after all.
Abigail went to meet the army and
draw their attention away from Nabal.
She knew David had murder in his heart
for these evil, wicked men.
However, it was not David but God Himself
who killed Nabal.
This godly act left Abigail free to marry
David if she so pleased.
Later, Abigail and David got married
and lived in Ziklag.
Later, when David returned home
after fighting a battle,
David found their home destroyed by the
Amalekites, their enemy.
But even worse, Abigail and another wife
had been kidnapped too.
Feeling such great loss, David fell humbly
on his knees.
After praying, David's feet didn't drag.
He went looking for both wives
and found the two.
David learned that he loved Abigail
more than his earthly treasures
and all his many herds of cattle.
The Bible says where your treasure is,
your heart is too.

Abram, son of Terah and uncle to Lot,
was a pagan born in the land of Ur.
God told Abram to leave Ur and move onward
as He led the way.
The Bible says that Abram followed the Lord
by faith.
He never knew where he was going or how long
he would there abide.
These three men and their families and flocks
traveled on to Haran.
In Haran, Terah decided to stay, and Terah
lived there until he died.
But Abram and Lot kept traveling until they
came near Bethel.
There, Abram said it was time for him and Lot
to travel their separate ways
because both men had large herds of animals
needing much water
and land upon which to graze.
Unselfishly, Abram told Lot to choose where
he wanted to settle.
Even though Abram was the elder,
he allowed Lot to choose first.
Lot chose the more fertile land of Sodom;
Abram then chose Hebron.
Abram might have chosen second,
but God had for Abram a mighty plan.
God changed Abram's wife's name from Sarai
to Sarah, and Abram's name
was changed to Abraham.
God told Abraham to count the stars above
and the grains of sand below.
Mathematically, both were too numerous
to count, even though
Abraham looked as far as he could.
He tried his best.

He looked in all directions—north, south,
east, and west.
God said Abraham's descendants
would be just as many as these.
Since Abraham and Sarah had no son,
he wondered, *How could this be?*
Later, God told Abraham and Sarah
they would have a son.
Sarah laughed because she thought they
were too old to have a child.
But God said nothing was impossible for Him!
At one hundred years old, Abraham became
a father to baby Isaac.
The name Isaac means "laughter" as Sarah
had laughed at God's plan.
The family had a big feast to celebrate
the birth of their son.
Father Abraham became the patriarch
of Israel's innumerable clan.
With God all things are possible—
only believe; don't jump the gun
as Sarah did when she told Abraham
to go to Tamar, Sarah's servant girl.
Sarah was in a hurry, wanting Abraham to run.
Wait on God's perfect timing.
He's never too early or too late.
He's right on time, every moment,
and on every date.

Adam was the first human created from God's
own hand
from the dust of the ground in the newly planted
garden of Eden land.
God shaped him out of His own image we're told.
When God breathed the breath of life into him,
Adam became a living soul.

God brought the animals He had created
for Adam to name them, one by one.
He was to care for them, having no fear,
as they were all tame, you see.
Still Adam felt so alone, not having another
human being with which to be.
While Adam slept, God took one rib away,
performing the first surgery.
God created a soul mate for Adam.
Adam named the woman Eve.
God didn't create another man, Steve.
God planned for one man and one woman
to make up the first family.
God knows all about us. He's omniscient.
God knows our every need.
Supplying our every need, God is sufficient.

Amos was a prophet of Israel who warned
the Israelites about their sins.
His messages were mostly those from his
five visions of "glum and doom"
of what God could do about Israel's
disobedience to Him.
Amos wanted the people to believe there's
absolutely no room
for any other god in Israel, and furthermore,
anywhere else in the world.
Amos was adamant that there was only one
true God, Jehovah.
Amos prophesied that only through repentance
could Israel be saved.
However, Amos did admit that maybe God
had a remnant, just a few believers,
who could keep the bloodline in the house
of David flowing through
future generations.

Amos foresaw a pattern of people rebelling
and then pleading for God's salvation.
Does this sound familiar?
Are we any different today?
We're so blessed that our merciful God
loves us anyway.

Andrew, a brother to Simon Peter, was a follower
of John the Baptist
until he met Jesus at the Jordan River, where Jesus
came to be baptized.
Andrew heard John call Jesus, "The Lamb of God."
He hurriedly traveled back home to tell Peter
the exciting news.
Andrew had found the Christ.
He had met the Messiah face-to-face.
Jesus soon went to the lake where the brothers
were fishing.
Jesus said He would make them "Fishers of men"
instead.
Immediately, Andrew and Peter left their boats,
their nets, and their poles.
They left their families and friends to follow
their Master's wish.
Once on a mountainside, where a hungry crowd
waited for food,
Andrew found out that a little boy had two fish
and five loaves of bread.
He brought the lunch to Jesus, knowing Jesus
would know just what to do.
Jesus would pray and ask for God's blessings
on all the sisters and brothers.
That day, because of Andrew's faith in action,
five thousand people were fed.
Andrew showed us how to use our twos
and our fives

for sharing what we have to help others.
We have two eyes to see others' needs,
two ears to hear their pleas,
two hands (five fingers each)
to help carry their loads,
and two feet (five toes each)
to walk with empathy down their roads.
Only then, can we have full compassion
for their lives.

Angels brought a message about the promised
Son of Man.
It was told first to the Virgin Mary and then
to Joseph, her fiancé.
Later, Mary and Joseph would come
to understand God's perfect plan
that Jesus, the Savior of the world, would be born
in Bethlehem's stable.
After His birth, angels announced it to the lowly
shepherds first.
They began to sing glory to Jesus, the newborn King,
peace on Earth and mercy mild,
God and sinners reconciled.
Two years later, angels warned in Joseph's dream
of King Herod's law
that Jesus's family must flee to Egypt
lest they all would fall.
Angels know that our God is omniscient,
and He is more than able!

Anna, a prophetess, waited at the temple
with Simeon, who was told he would not die
until he saw the promised Messiah eye to eye.
On that special day, Jesus's parents brought Him
there to be dedicated to God
at their place of worship, the Jewish synagogue.

Follow Anna's example; go to church expecting
great and mighty things from the God of miracles.
It's really just that simple!

Apollos was a Jewish man in Alexandria
who was trained in the faith by Aquila and Priscilla.
He ministered in Corinth and was later sent to Achaia.
Apollos was willing to learn from his teachers
all he could,
so he was prepared to lead others in faith,
just as Jesus would.
You, too, can help win the lost. It's as easy as A, B, C
and 1, 2, 3.
1—Admit.
2—Believe.
3—Call on Jesus
to forgive you as you pray on your bended knee.

Aquila was married to Pricilla and they lived
in Greece at Corinth.
They, like Paul, were tent makers by trade
and soul winners at large.
Aquila and Priscilla traveled with Paul
to Syria and Ephesus.
Also, Aquila trained Apollos in the Christian faith
in great length.
When Paul needed a host, they allowed him
a place to stay free of charge.
True friends share whatever they have
to bless others in the name of Jesus.

Aristarchus was a Christian from Macedonia.
He traveled with Paul spreading the gospel
message to all who would listen.
Later he and Paul were sent to prison
because of their Christian beliefs.

He wanted everyone to serve the Lord
and go to Heaven at their death.
He wanted no one to be separated from God
by going to hell.
Would we be that bold for Jesus,
knowing we might end up in jail?

B

Barak was a son of Abinoam and Judge Deborah's
right hand man.
Because of Israel's sin, God had delivered Israel
to Canaan's King Jabin.
When Deborah sent for Barak to fight the Canaanites
led by General Sisera,
Barak refused to go into battle unless Deborah
agreed to go with him.
So they both fought along with an army of 10,000
men on Mount Tabor.
Israel's men faced General Sisera's army who had
900 iron chariots.
Wow! Making those chariots was a time consuming
work of very hard labor!
Soon Sisera's men were surrounded by Barak's men
and all were killed,
except General Sisera who ran away on foot.
Barak ran after him in hot pursuit, arriving at the
tent of a woman, named Jael.
Inside Barak found General Sisera lying in the tent,
already dead.
Jael had hammered a tent peg through
his sleeping head.
Barak was too late to claim the victory he should

have had, if he had not delayed.
Instead, two women claimed the defeat of the
Canaanites that day.
Early Hebrew poetry records this act by Jael
in the praise songs sung by Deborah and Barak.
When asked to do a job, don't offer any excuses.
Just do it. Be ready to act.
If you don't, it could cost you a blessing that God
intended for you.

Barnabas, also called Joses, was a Levite
from Cyprus, who traveled with Paul
to carry Christianity to the Gentiles.
Barnabas sold his lands and gave the money
to the Apostles.
He was there in Jerusalem when Stephen
was stoned to death for Jesus.
He fled with other Christians to Antioch
and ministered there with Paul.
He brought the converted Paul back to Jerusalem
and spoke up for him.
The Jerusalem Christians accepted the newly
converted Paul solely because of Barnabas'
positive and encouraging recommendation.
He gave a testimony for Paul.
Barnabas was known as an encourager to all.
Afterwards Barnabas traveled with Paul to Cyprus
without delay.
Also that's where they started one of the oldest
Christian churches.
It would be called the Greek Orthodox Church, today.
Later Barnabas broke ties with Paul over a young
missionary named John Mark.
Paul thought Mark was immature and behaved
inadequately.
Barnabas and John Mark then set off on their own

missionary journey.
Sometimes God divides people up, so more souls
can be conquered for Him.
Divide to multiply – It's God's Heavenly math!

Bartimaeus, blind for all his life, never able to see,
sat on the Jericho road begging for food,
just as he did every day.
When he heard that Jesus was coming down that way,
he cried, "Jesus, Son of David, have mercy on me."
Jesus said, "Receive your sight. Your faith has saved
you today."
How exciting for Bartimaeus to now see the faces
of all his family and friends.
Now he was able to get a job and provide
for himself.
How great it is to walk around and see different places.
Have faith in God. He watches over every person
on plant Earth.
He knows the number of hairs on our heads.
He knew our names before our births.

Baruch was a friend and a scribe for the
Prophet Jeremiah.
He was an educated man for his day,
able to listen carefully to the truth.
He was certainly not a false-telling sooth.
God inspired Jeremiah with His Word to be
written down for all the ages.
Baruch was to use a quill and ink
to write it down word for word on a scroll,
without adding to or taking away anything
from what Jeremiah had told.
Jesus warned in the last chapter (22)
of Revelation to not add words
to the prophesy in the Bible or God

will add from the disasters listed
in the Bible to your life.
Furthermore if we subtract from God's
prophecy in the Bible, then God
will take away our part in the Tree of Life
and the Holy City.
Be aware of this advice from our Lord!
His Word is inerrant and already complete!

Barzillai, a Gileadite, was from Rogelim.
He befriended David and his army
out in the wilderness.
Barzillai brought bowls and jugs,
blankets and beds,
as David's men were so tired, hungry,
and more than ready to be fed.
Barzillai brought wheat, roasted grain,
barley, and flour
to make bread for the soldiers to regain
their physical power.
He also brought beans and lentils,
honey and curds,
and cheese from the flocks and the herds.
Later as David was about to die,
he told his son Solomon, the next King,
to be generous to the sons of Barzillai,
to extend every hospitality to them.
Barzillai had been so kind to David when he
was running for his life from Absalom,
another son of David's out in the desert,
so desolate and bare.
Be generous to others. It is more blessed to share.

Benjamin was the youngest son of Jacob
and his beloved Rebecca.
His mother died at his birth leaving Jacob

alone to raise their son.
His older real brother Joseph had supposedly
been killed years earlier.
The father had been led to believe this when he
saw Joseph's bloody coat.
Father Jacob couldn't bear to lose another son
at any cost.
However God had a plan and had intervened,
and Joseph's life has been spared.
Actually Joseph had become second in command
to Egypt's Pharaoh.
Joseph was over all the food supply in the land.
He had stored all the grain.
Benjamin was kept at home when the other ten
step-brothers
left to go to Egypt to buy food during the famine,
a time of no rain.
The ten brothers proved to Joseph how they
had changed and Reuben asked for forgiveness
with great humility for himself and the others.
Joseph wept, forgave them, and sent for Benjamin
and Jacob to come and live in Egypt with him.
Finally together again with Jacob were both
of his favorite sons by Rebecca,
Joseph and Ben.
Traditionally, a Benjamin was the youngest,
more doted on son.
A Benjamin's mess was a larger portion
as Joseph directed that five times
more food be put on Benjamin's plate
than those of his brothers at the banquet.
God says we should forgive others their sins,
as often as seven times seventy,
then He will forgive us our sins.
Unforgiveness leads to anger and hate.

Bezaleel was a master craftsman and clerk
of the works for the Ark.
Bezaleel was chosen by Moses to carry out
the elaborate building plans
given by God to Moses on Mount Sinai.
Bezaleel made the Ark for the Covenant,
all its sacred furniture, ornaments,
implements, and garments make out of gold
and other precious metals.
He used his God given skills to work mightily
with his very own hands.
Each of us can use our talents for God's glory.
Our goal is not just for our own pie in the sky.

Boaz had a heart full of compassion, it's true.
He told his workers not to gather all the wheat,
but to leave some on the ground, enough for two.
Boaz wanted to provide enough for these poor,
hungry widow ladies to glean, bake, and then eat.
Later Boaz took one lady, Ruth, for his wife
at God's right time and they had their family.
Boaz and Ruth had Obed; Obed had Jesse;
Jesse had David; and so on.
This is the lineage of Jesus' blood line.
Before the marriage of Mary and Joseph,
the Holy Spirit had caused Mary
to become pregnant with a baby boy,
who is all God and all man.
He was to be named Jesus, meaning,
"The Savior of the World."
We Christians can be adopted as His children
and into His family,
if we repent, believe, and receive
what He did for us at Calvary.
The adoption policy has already been fulfilled
and signed in red blood.

It can only be activated when you request it
in faith in Jesus.
Then all believers can belong to the
Holy Christian brotherhood.

Boy (not named) willingly shared his lunch one day.
When the crowd got hungry, the disciples told Jesus
to send them away.
But Jesus told the disciples no, to feed them instead.
A little boy's lunch that his mom had packed
was all that was found.
In the bag were two fish and five loaves of bread.
Jesus looked to Heaven and blessed the little
boy's lunch.
Then He broke the bread and fish into pieces
and passed them around.
When everyone had their fill, twelve baskets
full were left on the ground.
So always be ready to give Jesus your all,
no matter how small.
As the song reminds us that, "Little is Much
When God is In It."
He will bless you abundantly in this life.
That's really a whole bunch.
In Heaven, He'll even let you wear a crown.

C

Caleb was sent out with eleven others
to spy out the Promised Land.
He and Joshua came back with a glowing report
of great riches on hand.
Caleb advised Moses that domination of Canaan
was a sure thing, come what may.
Ten spies said, "No, no way." Only two said, "Go ahead,
God will lead the way."
But the Israelites' lack of faith and unfounded fears
caused them to wander in the desert another
forty years.
All the doubting generations died there in the desert,
so close to the money!
Only Caleb and Joshua lived to enter the land
of milk and honey.
Don't listen to the world's view and lose out
on God's rich blessings.
Put God on your team; God deserves first priority.
God plus one equals a majority!

Centurion, an unnamed officer, led one
hundred men in Capernaum.
He was a Gentile; His family came from Rome.
Therefore he was not a Jew, but he

was their generous friend, indeed.
He had paid to build the Jews their synagogue
when there arose the need.
When his favorite servant lay sick and dying
at his home,
the centurion sent word to Jesus to come
and heal his slave.
Later the centurion said he was unworthy
for Jesus to be in his house.
So if Jesus could just say the words,
his servant would be made well.
That he, just like the Lord, was told
by another what to do,
then he gave orders to his soldiers
and servants, too.
Jesus said He had not seen such faith
as this in all of Israel.
So pray to God in the name of Jesus
and believe His will
shall be done on earth as it is in Heaven.

Christ, the one and only begotten Son of God,
came to earth as a little baby.
He grew up and willingly suffered, bled, and died
on Calvary's cross,
so we sinners would not have to suffer any loss.

Claudius Lysias was a chief captain of the Roman
guard in Jerusalem.
When he heard from Paul's sister's son,
Paul's nephew,
that forty Jewish men had vowed to not eat
or drink until Paul was dead,
the nephew was told not to breathe a word
of this evil plan to a living soul.
Of course, Claudius Lysias wanted to protect Paul,

another Roman citizen.
He hurriedly helped Paul leave the dangerous city
to go to Caesarea.
For his safety, Paul quickly left his home.
The group left at nine o'clock at night
on their journey, as Paul was to face
the enemy early the next morning.
Really, this was just a trick to ambush
Paul so they could get rid of him.
To surround Paul and keep him safe,
Claudius Lysias sent along two hundred
soldiers as a posse, or cavalry.
Also, he sent a letter written to Felix,
Caesarea's procurator, or governor.
This letter stated that Paul, a Roman citizen,
was rescued from a Jewish mob
who had turned violent over some religious
differences, only a minor squabble
before the Council, no criminal wrong doing, at all.
Governor Felix asked Paul which province
he came from in Rome.
Paul answered, "Cilicia," and was told Felix
would hear his case
when his accusers showed up, but for now,
he would be locked up
in King Herod's official quarters.
God will put a hedge of protection around
His children until God's work
in them on earth is completed
just as God has ordered.

Cleopas was a disciple walking with another,
possibly Peter, from Jerusalem
to Emmaus after the crucifixion of Jesus.
The two men were busily talking about what
had happened recently to them.

All of a sudden, they were joined by another
Man they didn't recognize.
He wanted to know what they were discussing
so intently.
He didn't seem to know what wonders
they had seen in Jerusalem.
Cleopas asked him if he were the only one
who didn't know and He asked what?
Cleopas told the Man all about Jesus
the Nazarene, from beginning to end.
Then the Man asked why they couldn't just
believe what the Prophets had said.
Next the Man started telling them
all the scriptures about Him,
from the Book of Moses, down through
to the Prophets.
When the three of them came to the edge
of the village, the disciples invited the Man
to eat a meal with them at Cleopas's house.
There the Man blessed the bread, broke it,
and passed it out to each of them.
Immediately they recognized the Man,
who was Jesus.
Suddenly Jesus disappeared from the table.
He was gone!
Stunned, they just sat around the table
recalling how His presence had felt like fire.
Hurriedly, they traveled back to Jerusalem
to find the other disciples.
The disciples told that Simon had seen Jesus.
Jesus was alive!
Cleopas and Peter told what had happened
on the road to Emmaus.
Instantly, Jesus appeared to them
and they were scared,
thinking He was a ghost.

He told them that a ghost doesn't have
muscle and bone as He did.
Jesus encouraged all the disciples
to touch Him, see His hands, and His feet.
The disciples still had trouble believing
He was really Jesus.
Next Jesus asked if there was any food
He could eat?
They offered him a left over fish and He ate
it right in front of their eyes.
Then Jesus shared more scripture with them,
telling them they were to be His first witnesses.
Cleopas and the eleven disciples were to stay
in the city until The Holy Spirit came
to equip them with power from on high.

Cornelius, a Gentile in Caesarea, was a
devout centurion and captain of the Italian
guard stationed there.
He had led all of his family to believe
and worship only God.
He helped those in need and was known
as a man of prayer.
One afternoon about three o'clock,
Cornelius had a vision.
An angel, just as real as a neighbor,
told him that because of his kindness
towards his neighbors and for his prayers,
God had noticed him. He had God's attention.
He was told to send to Joppa for Simon Peter,
who was staying at Simon the tanner's house
down by the sea to come preach in Caesarea.
Cornelius obeyed this dream, called for two
servants, and a devout soldier,
and told them everything very carefully,
down to each and every detail.

The three men traveled on to Joppa
as Cornelius had commanded.
Just as they arrived in Joppa, Peter
went up to the rooftop at noon to pray.
While there, Peter fell into a trance
about eating unclean or clean food.
By this time, the three men
reached the tanner's door.
Peter had been sent by the Holy Spirit
to the door.
Peter was told exactly what to say,
then invited the men inside.
Peter was told that a devout, respected man
in Caesarea had a vision
in which a Holy angel commanded that Peter
come there to speak.
The next morning Peter, along with some
friends, left Joppa
with the three men to return to Caesarea.
When they got too Cornelius's house,
there was a crowd waiting for him.
Cornelius got up and bowed down
on his face to worship Peter.
But, Peter pulled Cornelius up, and said
not to worship him.
Peter said he was only a man like any other
man, that between them, there was no difference!
Furthermore, Peter commented that it was special
that all of the men could relax and have fellowship,
even though, they were from different races.
God had shown this truth to Peter and that's why
he could come with no questions asked.
Next, Peter asked why he was sent for
and Cornelius relayed the vision.
Peter got so excited at this good news,
realizing this was certainly God's amazing truth.

Peter said it couldn't be plainer than this.
God seeks everyone!
God has no favorites – no race, no background,
no color, or creed.
Peter exclaimed that through Jesus Christ,
all are welcome to follow Him.
Then Peter told what God's Spirit
had done in Judea earlier, first in Galilee.
No sooner had the words come out
of Peter's mouth, when a mighty miracle
took place!
The Holy Spirit descended on Cornelius' house,
surprising the Jews.
Peter's Jewish friends couldn't believe
that the Spirit was poured out on these outsiders!
They began speaking in tongues and praising God!
Afterwards Peter baptized these non Jews in the
name of Jesus Christ.
If you have a dream or a vision, or just read
from God's word, the Bible, obey what it says
for you to do.
We only see what's right around us,
but God sees the big picture.

Crispus, a Jew, was a chief ruler
of a synagogue in Corinth.
He was the President of the meeting place
in the city.
Having heard Paul's preaching, Crispus
as well as his family
became believers, and they were all
baptized in the river by Paul.
This family encouraged Paul that all
his efforts weren't lost
on the Jews in Corinth, not at all.
Don't give up until God says its time

to move on to another mission field.
Then the Bible says to shake the dust
from your sandals and go.
Don't stop, don't pass go, don't yield.
Reaching just one for Jesus is well worth
the effort, no matter the cost.

Cushi was sent by Captain Joab to tell the news
of Absalom's death to his father, King David.
Another runner was also sent to David,
arriving there first.
However, this first man could not answer David's
question about whether Absalom was dead
or alive, because he had only seen a ruckus
in the forest.
However, Cushi had known exactly what
had happened to Absalom, and carried the news
that all of David's enemies were defeated.
Also, he told that he wished that all David's
enemies should end up like Absalom.
Cushi brought certain, factual news to his master,
King David.
Can we be trusted to carry the truthful news
of the gospel to please Jesus, our Master?

D

Daniel and three young friends were captured,
and taken captive from their homes, friends,
and families in Judah to Babylon.
Daniel's Hebrew name was changed to his Babylonian
name, Belteshazzar.
All three boys had to learn and speak the Babylonian
tongue.
So far, nothing in their lives had been any rougher.
When offered the royal diet, they bravely asked
for water and veggies to eat.
In ten days' time, Daniel and the others
were healthier and stronger
than if they had eaten the King's succulent meat.
They were to be trained for three years,
then placed in service for the King.
God gave them great wisdom, and Daniel could
even interpret dreams.
Daniel told the meaning of the dreams of a baker
and a butler, and both came true.
Three years later, the King had a dream,
and the baker remembered Daniel.
For the King, Daniel was made to tell the dream
as well as its meaning,
which was a whole lot tougher.

King Nebuchadnezzar was astounded that Daniel
could tell both parts,
and said Daniel's God was the God of all gods.
Soon the King had another dream, and called for Daniel.
The King was to have seven good years,
then seven bad ones.
Afterwards, the King learned that pride
goes before a fall.
When Daniel was an old man, he was called in
to see King Belshazzar,
who was Nebuchadnezzar's son,
to read the handwriting on the wall.
Its meaning was that the kingdom would be divided
and soon it would end.
The new Persian King made Daniel one of three
Presidents in the land.
Because of the other two Presidents' jealousy
of Daniel, they got the King to make a law
that people were to pray to the King three times a day.
Refusing this order, Daniel looked toward Jerusalem,
as he had always done, everyday.
Daniel was found guilty of praying to God
and thrown into the lions' den.
An angel came to the lions, closed their mouths,
and Daniel's life was saved!
God had a plan for the lives of Daniel
and his three friends.
God loves you and He has a plan to protect
and save you, too.
God can make a way when there's seems to be no way.

David, Jesse's son, was a lowly shepherd boy,
playing his harp, while watching his sheep.
God looked down and saw only a pure heart
in David, but not in his brothers.
God sent the Prophet Samuel to anoint David as king,

instead of the others.
David was anointed with oil and with the Holy Spirit,
at age fifteen.
While people look at the outside of a person,
God looks inside at the heart.
Soon, Samuel asked David to play his harp
for the gloomy King Saul.
Sure enough, the music made King Saul
feel much better, indeed.
At this time, Saul had no idea that David
would be the future king.
Later on, David went to check on his brother
in Saul's army.
He carried them bread and cheese and word
from their father.
While there, David heard the loud noise
from the giant, Goliath.
Goliath was nine feet tall and very scary
with all his armor from head to toe.
However, David was so brave, he would fight
Goliath without even a bow.
David picked up five smooth stones
and carried his slingshot and said,
"I come in the name of the Lord."
It only took one stone, thrown one time,
from his slingshot; That's all
it took to bring down Goliath and watch him fall!
That day, David won a great victory
for his country, Israel.
David brought Goliath's head to King Saul
as a trophy to God.
King Saul wanted David to not return home,
but to stay and fight
in his army, and live in the palace.
David became best friends with Saul's son, Jonathan.
David agreed and won many battles for Saul.

As the women sang, shouting that Saul
had killed thousands,
but David had killed ten thousands.
Saul became very jealous and wanted to kill David.
Soon, David had to escape through a window to freedom.
He went to the tabernacle, claimed Goliath's sword
as his own, and ate the holy bread there.
He fled to a cave, where later, four hundred
hungry men joined him as a loosely outfitted band.
They asked David to be their captain.
They served under his command.
Once, in another cave, David got close enough
to cut the corner of Saul's robe,
could have killed him but refused.
David said he couldn't kill God's anointed
king of Israel.
His men were confused.
After Saul died, seven years passed before David
was made King at age thirty.
Soon, there was more fighting with the Philistines,
just as before.
David prayed; God answered that David would hear
marching in the tree tops,
meaning that God would go ahead of David
and fight for him.
That day, David conquered the Philistines
after one hundred years of war.
While Saul had ruled, the Ark of the Covenant
had been hidden away.
Now, David wanted to bring it back to Jerusalem
without further delay.
David had a new ox-cart made to carry it.
Following behind the cart, the people sang,
danced, and made music to celebrate
the Ark's arrival on Mount Zion.
David used all his strength dancing before the Lord.

Jerusalem became known as the City of David.
One day, David told Nathan that he lived
in a cedar house, but God's Ark
was still in a tent.
That night, God told Nathan that David
had a heart to build His House.
Because David was known as a man of war,
he wouldn't be allowed to build the Temple.
David was to have a kingdom, his son would
also sit on its throne,
and be the one to build the House.
David's son, Solomon, was known as a man of peace.
David's kingdom would last forever.
David ruled Israel for thirty three years,
then died, and was buried in Jerusalem.
God might also choose you as a child to grow up
to do mighty works for Him!

Deborah was the only woman
to every judge Israel.
She had the Spirit of God within
her as she listened to the people's
serious problems,
as well as, their daily whims.
Her advice and solutions were given
in the hills of Ephraim.
When Israel was attacked by the
Canaanite King Jabin,
Judge Deborah sent for Barak
to come and raise an army.
However, Barak, not trusting God,
as he had been taught,
said he would not fight the Canaanites,
unless with him, Deborah fought.
She agreed to fight, but said Barak
would not get the honor that was due.

Deborah said Israel would win.
A woman would get the victory, too.
Sure enough, a run away, tired General Sisera
went to the tent of Jael.
While Sisera slept under a rug,
Jael put a tent peg through his head.
Two women, Deborah and Jael,
saved Israel from her enemies.
God uses both men and women,
boys and girls to carry out His mighty deeds.

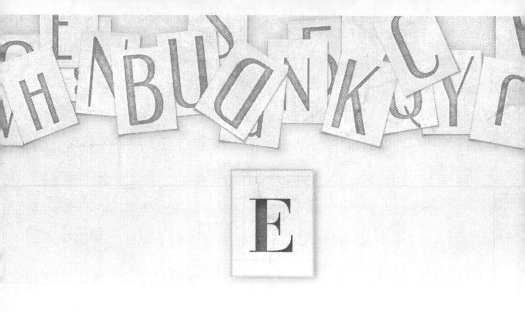

E

Ehud was one of the earliest Judges of Israel.
He was also a left-handed Benjamite.
Ehud was chosen by God to end
the eighteen-year slavery
of the Israelites from Eglon,
the King of the Moabites.
Ehud armed himself with a two-sided dagger
which was two feet long.
Carrying gifts to Eglon and telling him
that he had a secret to share alone,
Ehud got close enough to Eglon to thrust
the dagger into his fat belly.
Both the shaft and the blade went in so deep
that the belly fat closed in around the dagger,
and Ehud could not pull it back out of his stomach.
Ehud safely escaped and this deed
encouraged the Israelites to fight.
They killed ten thousand Moabites
at the crossing of the River Jordan.
Ehud was responsible for eighty years
of long awaited freedom from the Eastern quarter.
Ehud's successor, Shamgar, killed six hundred
Philistines from the West
with a ox-goad, delivering Israel once again

from any more slaughter.
It doesn't matter if you are a righty or a lefty,
your hand can be used to write,
draw, feed and bathe yourself, play a sport,
or make right a wrong
by defending innocent sons and daughters.

Eleazar, son of Aaron, succeeded him as Priest
and served alongside Ithamar, his brother.
Their other two brothers had been killed by God
for offering to Him a strange fire, not a proper
gift at all.
They had sacrificed to God in the wrong way, after all.
Eleazar served as senior Priest at Joshua's side
when the Israelites crossed the Jordan River.
Also, Eleazar was Priest when the promised land
was divided among the twelve tribes and the Levites
at Shiloh, and no others.
Eleazar's son, Phinehas, continued Aaron's line
in the priesthood.

Eli was a Priest and a judge of Israel,
serving in the temple at Shiloh.
One year at the temple, he heard Hannah
praying for a son.
When Hannah gave birth to a boy,
she named him Samuel.
When Samuel was old enough,
Hannah left him at the church with Eli.
Samuel was a comfort to the aging Eli.
As Samuel grew, he once heard a voice
calling in the night.
Thinking it was Eli, Samuel went to him
three different times.
Now, Eli knew it was God calling Samuel at his bed.
Eli taught Samuel how to answer the voice.

Samuel was to say, "Speak Lord, your servant
is listening."
Eli wanted to be told what God had said to Samuel.
Eli was to lose his sons and his priesthood.
Eli knew that whatever God did would be nothing,
but good.
Eli respected God's divine choices.
As Eli got older and now blind, he got word
that his sons were dead.
Even worse, the Ark in their care had been captured.
Hearing this news, Eli fell backwards,
breaking his neck, and died.
Parents of disobedient children have to suffer,
too, sometimes.
Be sure you obey God, Mom, Dad and others
in authority over you in the meantime.

Eliezer was a trusted servant to Abraham.
He was sent on a very important mission
by his master.
He was to find a bride for Isaac,
Abraham's son by Sarah.
His bride had to come from Abraham's
extended family in Ur.
She had to be a kinswoman from their ancestral
home – no other.
Isaac couldn't have a local bride from Canaan
who worshiped idols.
He gathered jewels, expensive cloth, gold,
and silver, no less.
With riches such as these, the young lady
would surely be impressed.
Eliezer loaded up several camels
for the long journey ahead.
He also carried people and animal food
and sleeping blankets for their beds.

During the trip, God helped Eliezer
to make a wonderful plan in his head.
When he came to a well for water,
whichever lady cam to him first
to offer him water, and then for his camels, too,
to ease their thirst,
would be God's choice,
just as if he were hearing God's own voice.
Later on, at a resting stop, near a well,
Eliezer saw such a girl as this.
She did exactly what Eliezer was looking for
in God's perfect plan.
Her name was Rebecca, a cousin to Isaac,
and Abraham's niece, their kin.
She invited Eliezer back to her home
where he met her father, Laban.
Her family accepted the gifts
that Abraham had sent.
Eliezer then enjoyed a feast
with Abraham's clan.
Laban gave Rebecca his blessing
to return with Eliezer to Canaan to be wed.

Elijah was a Prophet from God to King Ahab
and Queen Jezebel.
He told them to stop worshipping idols,
especially Baal.
Elijah said for them to repent, turn back,
and obey the one true God, or else.
There would be no water from Heaven –
not any rain, sleet, snow, or even hail.
The gods of Baal and our one true God
had a contest on Mount Carmel
to see whose god could rain down fire first,
and burn up their bulls.
Baal's 450 prophets prayed to their sleeping idols,

chanted, and cut themselves for six hours,
but to no avail.
Faithfully, Elijah's God sent fire from heaven
to consume, not only the wet sacrifice,
but also the twelve stones around the altar,
plus the trench water.
The people had agreed to obey the winner that day.
Obediently, they fell down on their knees
to worship and to pray.
God was victorious! In His mercy,
He forgave them of their sins
and sent rain upon their land.
Knowing agony and terrible defeat,
King Ahab left there in his horse drawn chariot.
Elijah left on his own two feet.
For seventeen miles, Elijah ran, arriving back
at the palace first, still completely dry.
However, King Ahab got drenched, arriving second,
probably mad as an old wet hen, and wanting to cry.
Only worship the one true God!
He says He is a jealous God; Don't serve another.
Therefore, don't put any other thing (idol)
in His rightful place, absolutely no other.

Elisha was a prophet who followed
after the Prophet Elijah.
He saw Elijah carried up to heaven
in a chariot of fire.
He watched Elijah's mantle fall to the ground
in a whirlwind.
Elisha picked up the robe, putting it to the test
at the Jordan River.
Would the robe separate the waters for him
as it had for Elijah?
Could he, too, walk across on dry ground
without getting wet?

Indeed, God did another miracle
as only He can deliver!
Reassured, Elisha knew God's anointing
would meet his needs.
God will meet all your needs, too.
He says He knows what you have need of
before you ever ask.
Ask, believing, God will always answer.

Elizabeth, was the wife of Zacharias,
and the mother of John (the Baptist).
She listened excitedly as Mary, her cousin,
told about the angel Gabriel's message that she
would have a special boy.
At the same time, Elizabeth's very own baby
inside her leaped for joy.
There's just something about that name, Jesus.
One day, every knee will bow and every tongue
will confess the name of Jesus.

Enoch, a man who walked with God,
prophesied to all those around, to not wait
but to obey and follow Him.
Enoch didn't die even when he was old.
Instead, God sent a chariot to carry him up
to the streets of gold.
Do you think God might send Enoch and Elijah
back to earth one day?
These two men never died a physical death on earth.
Could they be the two witnesses called to preach
for three years as a final warning
to the lost to repent before it's too late?
The Bible says that two witnesses will be persecuted
but God will protect them until their usefulness
in His plan has been fulfilled.
Only then will He allow the Godly witnesses to die

a physical death by their earthly enemies.
Then they can return to their Heavenly homes once again.

Epaphras was a church leader, teacher,
and Paul's close friend.
Paul wrote to the church in Colosse that the Message
of Christ taught to them by Epaphras was just as
powerful at that moment as it had ever been.
Paul said Epaphras was one reliable worker
for Christ, always dependable.
He's the one who taught them that the Holy Spirit
had thoroughly worked into their lives a Godly love.
Also, Paul called him a trooper, as he was tireless
in his prayers to the One above,
that the church would stand firm, mature, and
confident in everything
God wanted them to do, blessing them with great joy.
Paul wrote that he had watched Epaphras closely
and could report to Laodicea, Hierapolis, and Colosse
that he had worked hard for the believers.
Will you be thought of as a dependable, prayer warrior?

Epaphroditus was a messenger for Philippi
who went to see Paul in jail.
He brought gifts that Paul wrote were more
than enough, like a sweet-smelling sacrifice
roasting on the altar,
filling the air with fragrance, pleasing God to no end.
Epaphroditus knew that a personal delivery
of the gifts was more meaningful than any of the gifts,
themselves, he would send.
Paul wrote a letter to the church in Philippi,
thanking them by mail.
A personal touch makes any gift more valuable
to the receiver.

Esther, or Hadassah, was a cousin to Mordecai
from Shushan.
She was a Jewish girl whose name means, "Star."
When both her parents died, Mordecai raised her,
adopted her, as was God's plan.
She was very beautiful and went to the palace
to see Ahasuerus, the Persian King.
He was looking for a bride, both near and far.
At a banquet, Esther, helped by Hegai,
was chosen as Persia's new Queen.
Let it be known that when God's at work,
there's never any mystery.
While sitting at the palace gate one day,
Mordecai found out about a plot to kill the King
and sent word to Esther, who warned the King,
saving his life.
All these events are recorded in Persia's
written history.
When Haman came into power, the King
wanted everyone to bow down to him.
Of all the Jews, only Mordecai refused to bow
to Haman; He continued to resist.
He would only bow to worship God.
No matter who otherwise tried to insist.
Haman chose to punish all the Jews.
He thought himself too important to single out
just one man.
So one day, Mordecai heard that wicked Haman
wanted all the Jews killed on the thirteenth day
of the twelfth month – absolutely without any misses.
Mordecai told Esther to go to the King
and take a copy of Haman's death wishes.
He said that maybe she was placed in the kingdom
for such a time as this.
For three days, they each would pray.
Then she'd go, if even unto her woe.

Esther invited the king and Haman to have dinner
with her, not once, but two nights in a row.
The king granted her desire – to save her life
and the lives of all her Jewish kin.
Still today, the Jews celebrate Purim
and recall the story of Esther and Mordecai
and Haman's awful sin.

Eutychus, from Troas, was a young man in age.
He was sitting in a third story, open window seat
in a well lit room listening to Paul lead the worship
at a Sunday meet.
Well past midnight, Eutychus fell asleep and toppled
out of the window.
Eutychus was found dead, lying on the ground below.
Paul stretched out on top of Eutychus, and hugged
him hard, as if they had just met.
Paul said for them not to cry, that there was life
in Eutychus yet.
Paul then got up to serve the Master's Supper
and told faith stories until dawn.
Then, everyone left the meeting place to travel on
or to go back home.
Eutychus was very much alive and healthy,
free of his earlier death cage.

Ezekiel prophesied in Babylon about Israel's future.
God's Spirit took him to the "Valley of Dry Bones."
God asked Ezekiel if he thought these dry bones
could live?
Ezekiel responded that only God would have that
answer to give!
God told Ezekiel what He would do to let the people
know He is the Lord.
Ezekiel spoke the words to the dry bones just as he
had heard God's voice.

Suddenly, as the bones came together, there was a
rattling noise.
Next, muscle and sinew covered the bones without
needing even one suture.
Then Ezekiel spoke to the four winds as breath
entered into each lung.
Immediately, the bodies came alive, and they stood
on their own two feet.
God said He would free His people from captivity
by using His own tongue!
He would fill them with His Spirit and gather them
all together to meet.
These fully alive bodies will become the Nation
of Israel, in fact.
God wanted the people to know He had spoken,
and He was ready to act.

Ezra, a Jewish man and a scribe, lived in Babylon.
He studied the law; He taught the law.
But, most importantly, he kept God's law.
He gathered all the ancient writings
and for the first time,
the Old Testament scrolls were all together
as one big book.
He and the other Priests carried these scrolls
to Jerusalem
for them to have a look.
At their arrival, and to Ezra's great sorrow,
they found that many people,
including some Jews, were marrying people
who worshiped idols.
Their children couldn't speak Hebrew,
and they didn't know about God.
Ezra quit eating; He only wanted to pray.
As he prayed, some people gathered around,
and sat in the heavy rain.

Afterwards, Ezra sent all who had married
a foreigner away.
So many men with their families left Jerusalem
that day.

F

Father God, first person of the Trinity,
Creator of the universe with all its majesty,
Praises be to the glories above
that You looked down on us with such
merciful love!

G

Gamaliel was a learned and respected Pharisee
who sat on the Council.
He warned that the Apostles shouldn't be
handled too roughly by the Law.
Gamaliel believed that if the Apostles
were doing God's work, their reward
would continue as God saw fit.
Nothing could stop it!
It was God's call.
But, if they were doing man's work,
it would fall apart on its own accord.
Gamaliel said humans shouldn't mess
with God's Holy business.

Gideon, the wisest, most courageous man,
had the most faith of Israel's fifteen judges.
He dismissed many unnecessary men by allowing
those who didn't really want to fight to go home.
Gideon observed how the men drank water at the bank.
Those who leaned over to lap up water like a dog
were dismissed.
These men would be easy targets.
Those men who stayed on their knees and cupped
hands of water so they could still be alert

were selected for the assignment.
Gideon weeded out undisciplined men until he
had just 300 soldiers,
according to God's own perfect plan.
They gathered jars of clay with hidden lamps
and trumpets, that was all.
God told Gideon to use only these to defeat
the Midianites.
Afterwards, for forty years, Israel had peace,
with no enemy to fight.

Good Samaritan, as he journeyed down the road
toward Jericho,
didn't pass on by when he saw a hurt man.
This man had been stripped of his clothes,
hurt and robbed by some thieves,
and left half dead.
The Good Samaritan came where he was,
looked on him and had compassion.
He bound his wounds, poured in oil and wine,
set him on his own horse,
brought him to the inn, and put him to bed.
He took care of him, paid two pence,
maybe even more later to the inn's host.
Unlike the Priest, who couldn't be deviled
in his presence, and passed by
on the other side or the Levite,
who came and looked on him, then passed by, too.
The Good Samaritan gave the hurt man aide.
So then, who was his neighbor? What did Jesus say?
Of course!
It was answered – the one who showed mercy –
the one who did the most.
Jesus said, "Go and do likewise." The Good Samaritan
was so kind that day!
Be ye kind one to another. All lives matter,
don't you know?

H

Habakkuk was a Prophet during the time
of the seventh century BC.
At this time, God had allowed the Babylonians
to take over Israel.
He didn't understand how a godless nation
could take over a Godly one.
He asked God to condemn the ones
causing Israel's miseries.
He wondered if God knew what He was doing.
What was God's role?
He was depressed, thinking if they would ever
escape this captivity?
He voiced his feelings and his complaints,
and demanded God's attention.
Even though he had doubts, he did offer a glimmer
of hope, if only a mention.
The Old Testament book, Habakkuk, in our Bible
bears his name.
Unlike most Prophets, he boldly told his appeals
to God, without shame.
Do we sometimes question God?
Does God always make sense?
Like Habakkuk learned, we need to wait on,
listen to, and pray to God.

God sees the big picture; He has something good
for us in His sovereignty.
A commentary on Habakkuk's life was one
of the most valuable items
found in 1947 in the Dead Sea Scrolls.

Haggai was a Prophet who had a very important
mission on hand.
He was to get God's people to rebuild God's Temple
at God's demand.
He was obedient to God, knowing that rebuilding
the Temple itself
was just as spiritual as the activities that would
go on inside, later.
To accomplish his goal, he used nails and lumber,
mortar and brick.
The project lasted only three and one half months,
no more, and no less.
Most Prophets preached to the people about their
being sin sick.
It seemed Haggai's work was less spiritual,
and more physical in nature.
He wanted the place of worship to be safe, clean,
without any mess.
All jobs, whether we think they're great or small,
are spiritual in God's sight.
There's no ranking of greater than or lesser than
in God's equality (< >).
Whatever you're asked to do, be obedient, and work
in humility.

Hannah, the wife of Elkanah, had no child,
no girl or boy.
Because of her sadness, she often cried
as she prayed.
One year outside the tabernacle at Shiloh,

she begged God to just give her one little boy,
at least.
She promised she would give him back when he
got older to be a Nazarite Priest.
God answered her prayer in His good time
as He saw fit.
Baby Samuel was born into a loving,
waiting family unit.
After Samuel was weaned, Hannah kept her word.
She took him to the temple to help the aging Priest, Eli.
Hannah made a new, bigger coat for Samuel
to wear every year.
She watched him grow from afar but, in her heart
and in her prayers,
he was always very near.
Hannah honored the Lord God in her words
and in her deeds.
Don't ever make a promise that you don't intend
to keep.
Your word is your bond!

Hezekiah, the son of Ahaz, repaired the temple doors
as his first project when he became the King of Judah.
After that, he had the temple cleaned, and even more,
he removed the idols from within its midst,
and had them burned in the dump.
He told the Priests their ancestors from Judah
and Jerusalem
had forgotten all about worshiping Him.
They had quit offering incense and burning sacrifices
to Israel's God.
They had ceased oiling the lamps, had closed
the temple doors, and went on their merry way.
These ancestors whose families were taken captive
were killed by the sword,
or in others ways they died.

In his heart, Hezekiah wanted an agreement with God,
so His anger would go away.
So for two weeks, the Priest cleaned, made offerings,
and ministered to God until His house was purified.
Later on, King Hezekiah's kingdom was invaded
by the Assyrians, their enemies.
Hezekiah simply cut off their water supply,
strengthened the Jerusalem wall,
and made many new weapons for the battle to be.
Then King Hezekiah called the people together,
saying, "Don't be afraid.
There will be more with us than with them."
Soon messengers came from Assyria shouting terrible
things about God.
Because of this, Hezekiah and Isaiah prayed together
to Him.
God sent His angels to kill Assyria's head warriors
within their own camp.
Their king had to return home in shame, eventually
killed by his own sons.
God's people in Jerusalem were saved and got much
needed rest.
Hezekiah became famous in all the nations
because of God's great quest!
Later on, the Assyrians attacked Judah once more.
King Hezekiah became sick, and the Prophet Isaiah
came to visit, speaking God's message.
The King was told he would not get well,
to prepare for his death,
but, Hezekiah said he was not ready from this life
to depart.
He prayed and cried out to God to remember all he
had done during his reign.
He said he'd been faithful, serving his God
with his whole heart.
The God of David, his ancestor, heard his prayers

and saw his tears.
God changed His mind – He would heal Hezekiah
and add to his life another fifteen years,
plus save the city under attack in Judah-Jerusalem.
So he could really believe Hezekiah wanted a sign
from Him,
Isaiah said Hezekiah could choose the sign
about time to ease his mind.
Did he want the sundial to gain or to lose
ten minutes of time?
Hezekiah said since the sundial time always
goes forward,
he wanted the shadows to go backward for him.
As Isaiah cried out to God, the shadow
moved backwards exactly ten minutes,
no less, no more.
After only three days, King Hezekiah's health
was restored.
God can make time go backwards, go forward,
or just stand still.
Our God can do miracles – for Him, it's no big deal!

Hilkiah was a Priest in Jerusalem during the reign
of King Josiah.
When the temple was being repaired in 621 BC,
he found a book of Law.
Some think it could be the Book of Deuteronomy
in our Old Testament.
King Josiah agreed with Hilkiah that the law
should be followed.
Together, they wanted the beliefs and manners
from long ago to be revived.
Centuries later, this book was used to make
strict laws and rituals for Priests.
Israel made a constitution for Priests based
on what Hilkiah had found.

Hilkiah was the father of the prophet, Jeremiah.
Treasure can be found in the trash if you
are willing to look for it!

Hiram was the King of Tyre.
He was also a friend of David and his son, Solomon.
Hiram also did business with King Solomon.
He supplied the cedars and firs for the building
of the Temple in Jerusalem.
In exchange for these, Hiram received food
and oil from King Solomon.
Hiram built King Solomon and his wife
a beautiful palace for their family home.
The two Kings' navies sailed together to Ophir
at the far end of the Red Sea
to find gold, timber, and precious stones.
Both Kings loved their luxuries and monies
with which to be able to buy or to barter or to hire.
It is thought that Hiram built a causeway
between Tyre, an island, and the mainland.
It seems God gave Hiram a talent for building
and getting riches.
Hiram was blessed by God because he served God
in the building of the Temple.

Hosea was a Prophet of love, real love, God's love.
Hosea's story is a lived parable in an Old Testament
book in the Bible.
Hosea was told by God to marry Gomer,
who was a bad woman.
They were told to have children, to become a family.
God named each child and told its parallel meaning
to Hosea and for Israel.
This story was to show how much God loved Israel,
even with all her flaws.
God seeks us when we are in a bad state of sin,

disobeying His Laws.
Our sins break His heart, but He loves us anyway.
God loves us even when we're unlovely.
This love can't be bought!
God keeps drawing us to Him, so we can repent,
and worship Him.
Then, we can have a relationship
with the real God of love.
And then, we can better love
our neighbor as we ought.

Holy Spirit, third person of the Trinity,
is also the Comforter sent by God
in the name of Jesus.
He will teach us all things; He will bring
all things to our remembrance,
so that the words said by Jesus unto you
will always hold fast.

I

Isaac, son of Abraham, saw his father's great faith
one day.
On the mountain of Moriah, Abraham was asked to slay
his only son as a gift to God.
Isaac innocently asked where was the lamb
for God's gift?
As Isaac was laid on the altar by his father Abraham,
Abraham answered that God would provide a lamb
and raised his knife.
Just then, an angel stopped Abraham, for indeed,
God had provided a ram.
The ram was stuck in a bush just waiting to be used
as a substitute for his son's life.
What a realistic picture of what God did on the cross
for us all.
God's only Son, Jesus, became our very own
sacrificial Lamb!
When Isaac got grown, he married Rebekah,
his cousin.
They had twin sons – Jacob and Esau.

Isaiah was told by God to be His Prophet,
to speak His words to His people, even though,

they won't listen; They won't understand.
They won't turn to Me and be healed by My hand.
They will be like a tree cut down to a stump
but out of its roots, a new tree will grow.

J

Jacob was the younger twin son of Isaac and Rebecca.
His older twin was Esau, and they were born
posed to fight.
Jacob was born clutching Esau's foot.
Jacob was his mother's favorite son.
Esau was his father's first choice.
When Isaac got old enough to give his blessing
to his older son,
he was already losing his sight because of aging eyes.
With his mother's help, Jacob dressed as Esau
and brought stew and tricked his father.
Jacob received the blessing, but soon afterwards
he had to leave home in haste.
Jacob traveled toward Uncle Laban's house,
but stopped for the night.
He dreamed there was a ladder with angels
going up and down.
When he awoke, he poured oil on his headstone
for an altar,
and called it, "Bethel, the Lord's House."
A rock became a pillow for Jacob's head.
The same rock became a pillar of remembrance
for Jacob's heart.
Jacob arrived at his Uncle's house and soon fell

in love with his cousin Rachel.
He agreed to work seven years to wed Rachel
but, he got deceived by his uncle,
reaping what he had sewn to his brother, Esau,
back home.
Now, he had married Leah, the older sister
who wore a bridal veil to cover her face.
Jacob was tricked into working another seven years
for Rachel's hand.
There was nothing Jacob could do; He had no voice.
This was another example of a deceit by sight.
In all, Jacob worked twenty years for Uncle Laban
but now, he wanted to return to his homeland.
Jacob sent many gifts ahead to Esau
to soften his heart toward Jacob.
That night before the reunion, while dreaming,
Jacob wrestled with an unknown man,
who couldn't throw him. Jacob was left with a limp.
Jacob thought this Man was God Himself.
God renamed Jacob-Israel.
The next day, the forgiving Esau and Jacob
were reunited as brothers.
Jacob had twelve sons by two different wives.
His favorites were Joseph and Benjamin by Rachel.
Through his sons, Jacob-Israel became the forebear
of the Israelites.
Israel was the father of the twelve tribes
and the Levites.
Be careful how you treat others.
It may come back to bite you and leave a lasting mark.

Jairus was a synagogue leader who sent for Jesus
when his twelve year old daughter got sick.
When Jesus and three of His disciples arrived
at Jairus' home,
they were told that the girl was dead.

Jesus said she was not dead, only sleeping
on her bed.
The neighbors laughed at His words.
They were sent outside to give Jesus
some peace and quiet.
Then, Jesus brought Jairus' daughter back
from a life of doom.
Jesus told His disciples and the parents not to tell
what had happened inside the room.
They were to keep it private among themselves.
Unbelievers can mistake a miracle
for a magician's trick.

James, a fisherman and a disciple of Jesus,
was a son of Zebedee.
He was also called, "James the Great."
Maybe, he was a big man, you see.
Along with his brother John, and Peter,
he belonged to an inner circle
of the twelve disciples, called
"The Sons of Thunder."
Jesus loved all His disciples, about that,
there's not any wonder.

James the Less was thought to be Jesus' brother
or cousin.
There was some type of family tie that made them
very close knit.
He wrote the book of James in the New Testament
in our Bible.
For refusing to denounce Jesus, he was stoned
and clubbed to death.
He was faithful until he took his very last breath.
What an example of great courage!
Can anyone dare to rival?
Maybe James was a small person in size,

but in showing boldness, he was so much more.
He would absolutely never compromise.

Jeremiah was called the weeping prophet.
However, he told the people not to weep
at King Josiah's death,
but, to weep for Josiah's righteous son who
was going away from Judah, never to return.
Josiah's evil son became the king and led
the people back to idol worship,
as their earlier ancestors had done.
Jeremiah warned the new king against such actions.
The new king tried to have Jeremiah killed.
For awhile, some friends wanting to save Jeremiah,
helped him hide.
In his absence, his friend Barack read to the people
the prophesy to be fulfilled.
Later, soldiers took Jeremiah's scroll to the king
and had it read to him.
The king burned the scroll as it was read, even through
his advisors opposed this decision.
They knew Jeremiah was a Prophet of God
who spoke only His word.
This king was soon overtaken by his enemies,
later killed, and his body thrown out of Jerusalem.
No grave did anyone dig.
Much later, Jeremiah had, "A Vision of the Figs."
When God asked what did Jeremiah see,
the response was that he saw two baskets of figs,
not one or three.
Some were very good to eat; Others were very bad,
not fit to even be tried.
Only God could explain the meaning of Jeremiah's
vision.
The good figs represented the captives
taken to Babylon.

The bad figs symbolized the people left in Jerusalem,
even its King Zedekiah and his princes, and all
his people, everyone.
These would suffer plagues and famine
until they all died.
Happily, Jeremiah wrote of God's plan
to the captives in Babylon.
These people were to build houses, plant gardens,
marry, and have kids.
For God would bless them and take care of them.
There should be no fears.
He would return them to their homeland in peace
after seventy years.
He would be their God; They would be His people.
His mercy never ever wavered.
God only wanted to offer peace and kindness
to the good figs he favored.
Another time, Jeremiah warned King Zedekiah
to go with the Babylonians.
If he stayed, he would be killed, either by famine
or in battle.
This prophesy angered the king who threw Jeremiah
into a muddy, prison pit, and left him there to die.
An Ethiopian, Ebedmelech, asked permission
to rescue Jeremiah.
To get Jeremiah out of the pit,
he used very strong ropes.
Jeremiah was freed and given a choice
where he would abide.
First, he chose to live in Abraham's land of hope.
Later, he decided to move to Egypt where the Remnant
of God would settle.
Jeremiah prayed for the people's sins and wept
many, many tears
during the reign of kings in Judah over a vast period
of four hundred years.

Jesse was descended from Adam>Seth>Shem>Boaz.
He was the father of David and eleven other sons.
He became the ancestor of the royal Messianic line
of Judah down to Jesus.

Jesus, God the Son,
second person of the Trinity,
is our Lord and Savior.
One day, at the name of Jesus,
every tongue will confess
and everyone will bow the knee.
Jesus is King of Kings and Lord of Lords.
Blessed be the name of the Lord!
Sing His praises or else, the stones will cry out.
Clap your hands or give a shout
to Hosanna in the highest heaven!
To all who praise Him, He will surely bless.

Joash, as a baby, was hidden in the temple
for his safety by his Aunt.
At the age of seven, he was brought out of the temple
by Jehoida, the Priest.
A crown was placed on Joash's head as the people,
from oldest to least,
sang praises and shouted, "Long live the King."
This act allowed David's royal family to rule again
in Judah.
Joash, the seven year old king, made his first
royal decree.
He may have stamped it with his royal ring.
His first job would be to repair Solomon's temple.
Outside the temple doors, Joash placed a box
for the donations.
Joash didn't need to beg or to rave and rant.
The people gladly gave of their money
to fill up the box or chest.

Workers were hired to repair the Lord's house
on a timely rotation.
All of Judah worshipped there until the Priest died.

Job was a man who lost everything he owned:
his family, his animals, and his lands.
Job never blamed God; Job never said a swear word
or a curse.
His wife couldn't understand and asked if things
could be any worse.
But, Job knew in his heart that he would always
put God first.

Joel was a Prophet who said that God was always
at work on a daily basis.
He wanted God's message to be told down through
all the generations to all the different races.
He wanted the people to know that not a single day
went by,
without their having to deal with God in some matter,
whether big or small.
People should make all their decisions seeking
God's guidance, after all.
He told the story of how locusts destroyed the crops
in Israel,
as God's judgement for their sins of disobedience
and not worshiping Him.
The army of locusts devoured everything in their paths,
causing great loss.
However, the people were given a second chance
to repent before they died,
so their remaining days on Earth could be satisfying
to them, and pleasing in God's eyes.

John the Baptist, a cousin, and the forerunner
of Jesus,

lived in the desert, wore animal skins,
and ate wild locusts.
He preached about the coming Messiah
who was mightier than he.
As Jesus came toward John that day
at the Jordan River,
John recognized Jesus as, "The Lamb of God."
Later, while John was baptizing in the Jordan River
any new believers,
Jesus asked to be baptized, too.
As Jesus was baptized, the Holy Spirit came down
upon Jesus in the form of a dove.
God spoke saying, "This is my beloved Son."
John was content to be second best.
He knew Jesus was to be the real focus.
John said he was unworthy to even unloose
Jesus' shoes.
John said he must decrease,
while Jesus must increase.
Knowing your place in God's kingdom
by seeking His face,
offers everything to gain
and absolutely nothing to lose!

John, the son of Zebedee, was a fisherman.
He became an apostle of Jesus, "The Great I Am."
John, his brother James, and Peter
were in Jesus' inner circle of very close friends.
John was also known as the beloved disciple.
John was told by Jesus at Calvary
to care for His mother, Mary.
What an awesome command!
To be entrusted by the Master of the universe
to oversee His precious Mother's care
would be a place of honor for most.
This request could cause some to boast.

Some would puff up their prideful chests.
John undertook this task with tremendous love
and with the deepest humility.
John showed both Jesus and Mary respect
by saying, "Yes, Sir and Yes, Ma'am."

John was the author of the fourth book
in the New Testament.
The book of John begins as does Genesis
with, "In the beginning ..."
John points out that God spoke into being
both creation and salvation.
John says Jesus was and is the Word of God
in human flesh at His birth.
John reminds us that our words
make a huge impact on this Earth.
With them, we can accept or reject Jesus,
choosing life over separation.
John says that Jesus speaks salvation
into us as we voice, "I believe."
Let's make every opportunity for the lost
to hear God's Holy Word.

John of Patmos was a first century pastor
and also a poet, you see.
John had a vision, "The Revelation,"
on a Sunday while at worship
on an island called Patmos
on the Mediterranean Sea.
John was in charge of a circuit of churches
on the mainland.
John's main task in this position was worship.
None other should rival.
John wrote down his vision in the Book of Revelation
which is the last book of the New Testament
in our Holy Bible.

John believed worship shapes who we are in relation
to the Almighty God.
John warned that if we neglect worship, our nations
will suffer, by and by.
Satan hates worship, the world is hostile to it,
and times are cruel to worshipers
on this earthly sod
where we trod.
Yet, John insisted in Revelation that worship
be continued, even though,
some may be persecuted for their beliefs,
and some may even die.
John quotes in the last verse, "Even so Lord Jesus,
come quickly."

John Mark wrote the second book in the
New Testament in 70 AD.
It is the shortest one of the four gospels,
but, maybe, it is the oldest.
Mark seemed to be in a hurry to tell
the full gospel story.
He was passionate about the life of Christ
and His ministry.
He wrote of Jesus' birth, life, death,
resurrection, and ascension into Heaven.
Also, only Mark's gospel tells of a lone
follower who wore a white robe
around him at Jesus' arrest.
The man was attacked and forced to flee.
Did Mark write himself into that account?
Mark wanted us to know that Jesus seeks
to save us above all else!
Mark had a vision of the gospel
going around the globe.
Don't waste any precious time.
God is on our side! Never doubt!

Jonah was sent to Nineveh by God
to warn the people there about their sinfulness.
Jonah disobeyed and went his own opposite way
in a boat.
There causing trouble, the sailors threw him
overboard as that was Jonah's wish.
Instantly, he was swallowed by a very large fish.
Jonah lived inside the fish for three very long days
and nights.
Finally, the whale vomited him out onto dry land.
Jonah was now eager to follow God's plan.
Sometimes, God uses extreme means to make us
see the Light.

Jonathan was King Saul's son.
When David came to live in the palace with his family,
they became best friends in good times, as well as,
in times of sorrow.
To show his friendship Jonathan gave David
his favorite bow and arrow.

Joseph, as a boy, was given a coat of many colors
by his father, Jacob.
This made his brothers very jealous, indeed.
Also, he had dreams of his younger brothers
bowing to him on their knees.
Once when Joseph carried food to the brothers,
they had a wicked plan.
They stole his coat, put him down a well,
and then sold him to a caravan.
What they meant for evil God turned it into good.
Joseph went to Egypt, gained favor with Pharaoh,
and was put second in command.
Later on, after a famine, the brothers were sent
by Jacob to Egypt land.
Knowing not Joseph was their brother,

they did bow to him.
They showed they'd changed their hearts,
and asked for forgiveness.
Joseph forgave them, told them all to come,
and live with him,
and bring their father, Jacob, and especially,
his little brother, Ben.

Joseph was a descendant from the royal line of David.
He was a carpenter from Nazareth and was engaged
to the Virgin Mary.
He was told by Gabriel in a dream that it was okay
to marry Mary, after all.
He was told Mary's baby was from the Holy Spirit,
to name the baby, "Jesus."
Jesus means "He will save the people from their sins."
What a miraculous CALL!
Joseph didn't quite understand. Yet he trusted
God's perfect plan.
He became Mary's husband and soon,
they traveled ninety miles to their homeland.
They were required to pay their taxes
and be counted in a census in Bethlehem.
Finding no room in the inns, Joseph and Mary
had to have a place to stay.
The innkeeper said he only had a barn or stable left,
but they were welcome to his only available shelter.
Inside, they saw donkeys, cows, and sheep feeding
and lying on the hay.
What a humble birthplace for the Promised Messiah,
God the Son!
While there, Joseph witnessed the birth
of the Son of Man.
Mary wrapped Jesus, the baby, "I Am"
in a soft swaddling cloth.
And Joseph laid Him gently into the animals'
feeding trough.

Joseph of Arimathea was a wealthy man
in Jerusalem where he owned a plot
of land nearby where Jesus was crucified.
Joseph didn't know what the Jews
had planned to do with the body
after Jesus died on the cross.
Joseph went with Nicodemus
to ask Pilate for Jesus' body
so He could have a proper burial.
They anointed the body with oil
and wrapped it with a piece of linen.
What a kind gesture it is to care
for a friend in life but even more so,
caring for a friend or their family
after a death.
At this sad time loved ones
can feel such a terrible loss.

Joshua became the leader of the Israelites
after the death of Moses.
He was chosen by God to lead the people
across the Jordan River.
But first, he chose two wise and brave spies
to check out the city of Jericho.
The city had to be taken before the land, you know.
The Israelites could look across and see
the city walls.
At this time of year, the spies had to swim
in the overflowing Jordan River
to reach Jericho, for Israel had no boats.
The spies spent the night at the house of Rahab
who hid them on her roof.
For her help, she asked that her family
be spared in the takeover of the city.
She dropped a scarlet rope from her window
to let the spies escape.

Rahab was assured of her family's safety
if from the window the rope
remained for the Israelites to see it.
That was her only hope.
The spies came back and gave their report.
The Israelites packed to travel.
When it was time for the Israelites to cross
the river, the Priests, carrying the Ark
of the Covenant, stepped into the water first.
While their feet remained in the water,
the entire nation of Israel crossed over onto dry land.
When the Priests stepped out of the water,
it began to flow again, to beat the band.
While the Priests blew their trumpets, the Ark
would be carried around the city of Jericho once a day
for six days.
On the seventh day, they were to march
seven times around.
As Joshua ordered, they people shouted,
and the walls of Jericho came tumbling down!

Josiah, Amon's son and Manasseh's grandson,
was crowned king at the young age of eight.
He began to seek after God early in his life,
rather than waiting too late.
He cleaned out the land of idols at age twenty.
No king in Judah had ever done so much good
for so many.
He even went outside of Judah to complete
his list to do,
and even dug up the bones of Priests
who worshipped the idols and burned them, too.
He even found the temple at Bethel,
north of Jerusalem, where an idol of a golden calf
had been set up two hundred years earlier.
He burned the Priests' bones upon their altars

and crushed them into dust.
Also, he found the grave marker of the prophet
sent by God to the evil King Jeroboam when he
was offering incense to the golden calf.
He said to let the prophet's bones not be moved,
just let them rest.
What Josiah was doing today had been prophesied
many years ago.

Jubal was a brother of Jabal and son of Lamech
and his first wife, Adah.
He was the very first harpist and organist
referred to in Bible research.
He was the ancestor of those who made musical
instruments and music.
Jubal knew about the musical sounds
and which notes to put in every measure.
How wonderful that Jubal used his gifts
and talents for our Lord's pleasure!
What a blessing to worship our God
in the playing and in the singing of hymns
with glorious praises at home, or in church!
The Bible tells us that if we don't praise Him,
then the rocks will cry out.
No matter, what part you sing:
soprano, base, tenor, or alto,
whether in a quartet, a trio, a duet, or a solo,
in a choir or in an orchestra,
use what talents you've been given to play
or to sing as unto the Lord.

Judas, a Christian disciple, owned the home
in Damascus on Straight Street
where Saul stayed after his blinding experience
on the road that day.
While there, Saul thought about all

that had happened to him along the way.
Before this trip, he'd had Stephen stoned
to death in Jerusalem.
Saul had even come to Damascus to persecute
Christians, all of them.
But on the road, he'd heard the voice of Jesus
speaking to him asking why he was hurting
and killing His followers – WHY?
He stayed at the home of Judas for eight days,
being changed on the inside to be more like Jesus.
This conversion was Saul's salvation, spiritually.
Then, Ananias placed his hands on Paul's eyes
as God had demanded.
God's miracle enabled Paul to see again physically.

L

Lazarus was a brother to Martha and Mary,
and they all lived in Bethany.
Jesus loved Lazarus, Martha, and Mary.
They were special friends, all three.
One day Jesus got word that Lazarus
was ill, but sleeping, and getting better,
on the road to recovery.
However, Jesus knew Lazarus
was dead, not asleep,
nor had he dozed.
Heading toward Bethany, Jesus
heard that Lazarus had been dead
for four days, already.
Jesus saw Mary and Martha walking
toward Him, looking very sad.
Both said that their brother would
not have died if Jesus had been there.
The three of them met some mourners,
and Jesus wept for His friend, too.
Then, Jesus went to where Lazarus
was buried, told them to roll away
the stone in front of the tomb.
But, Martha said not to do it because
the body would smell awfully bad.

Jesus insisted, and then called Lazarus
to come forth from the dead.
Instantly, Lazarus obeyed and came out
of the tomb in his grave clothes.
Jesus proved that He had power
over death,
first with Lazarus in Bethany,
but later on, power over His own
death when from His tomb, Christ arose!
There's a song about Jesus not crying
because Lazarus had died but, because
He had called Lazarus back.

Little children, red and yellow,
black and white,
they are so very precious
in His sight.
They were brought by their parents
to Jesus for Him to give them
His loving touch.
They knew He loved their children
so very much.
The disciples wanted Jesus
to send them away.
But what did He say
to the disciples that day?
Jesus said the truth-
we must be like these little
ones, sitting on His knees.
For the kingdom of God
belongs to such as these.
Then, He hugged the big kids
and the little, tiny babies.

Lois, a very wise grandmother,
taught young Timothy the Torah.

Up on the rooftop, they would go.
Everyday they studied the scrolls
for more scriptures to know.

Luke, a medical doctor by trade
knew the medicine of his day.
But he learned from Jesus
how to cure man's deadly disease.
Luke prescribed repentance of sin,
and confessing often on your knees.

Lydia, a seller of purple cloth,
used regular thread to sew and stitch
the poor peoples' clothes.
At the riverside, she met her friends
for Bible study and prayer.
She knew broken hearts
needed the Savior's mending
using only His tender love and care.

M

Malachi wrote the last book in the Old
Testament in our Bible.
He recorded cause and effect events
from the God-of-the-Angel-Armies.
Sometimes, we tend to forget about God
when things go well for you and me.
Other times, we have to search for God
when things get tough and lonely.
God has never moved away from us,
God's created human race.
Malachi warns us not to wait on a crisis
to seek God's face!
He ended his book reminding his readers
about Moses' truths from the past,
and Elijah's truths for the future.
Both point us to keep worship a priority.

Manasseh, the son of Hezekiah, became king
at age twelve.
He did evil for many years, leading his followers
in doing evil, as well.
After he was captured, bound in chains,
and tormented by the Assyrians,
Manasseh repented and turned back to God

in Babylon.
God heard his prayers and returned him
to his kingdom in Jerusalem to rule.
Now safe, he destroyed all the idols
around him in the land.
He began to worship God, the only One
who is true.
He commanded Judah to serve only God, too.
He reigned as king of Judah for fifty-five years.

Manoah was from Zorah and from the tribe
of Dan.
He and his wife had no child.
She was a barren woman filled with shame.
An angel of God came to visit her and said
she would have a son.
The angel of God stated some things
that from her were required.
She could not drink beer or wine,
nor eat anything unclean, ritually.
Also, no razor would ever touch his head.
He would be God's Nazarite from his birth,
and he would deliver Israel from the Philistines,
their enemy.
The wife told her husband the good news
from the angel of God.
Manoah prayed that the angel would return
to tell them how to raise their child.
God answered his prayer, sent the angel
back to the wife, then to Manoah.
Manoah asked about the boy and his work.
How could they help?
Concerning the boy's discipline,
should they be bold or be mild?
The angel of God repeated the requirements
for the wife.

Then they wanted to repay his kindness
to them by fixing a meal.
A young goat could be prepared for which
they would gladly dine.
The angel said he couldn't eat their food,
but they could offer a Whole-Burnt-Offering
to God, if they so desired.
Then Manoah asked the angel his name.
Manoah wouldn't understand,
he was told.
Next, Manoah took the kid and the Grain-Offering,
and sacrificed them on an altar made from a rock.
As the flames rose up, so did the Angel of God
toward Heaven ascend.
Instantly, Manoah and his wife bowed facedown
to the ground in awe!
They never saw the Angel of God again,
after that sacred moment with Him.
Now, Manoah knew this was God's Angel,
and he was scared of Him.
Manoah's wife assured him that God
accepted their offerings,
and gave them the announcement
of their son's birth, after all.
Later their son, Samson, was born
and God blessed him as he grew to be strong.

Martha, the sister of Mary and Lazarus,
felt she must prepare
for a visit from Jesus,
their most special dear friend.
Martha had cooked and cleaned
without any help from Mary.
Now, Mary had sat near Jesus,
carefully listening to Him talk.
Mary was totally focused on Jesus.

To all others, she was totally unaware.
When Martha asked Jesus
did it bother Him at all?
He answered that Martha shouldn't worry
about things unnecessarily.
Mary had chosen the most important thing:
"Just loving Me!"

Mary, the Virgin maiden, was visited
by the Angel Gabriel.
She was chosen by God above all the other women,
to birth His Son, then later watch Him die.
Mary pondered all these things in her heart,
knowing she had a truly blessed part!

Mary was a sister to Martha and Lazarus.
The tree of them lived in Bethany.
At Simon's house, as Jesus taught the scriptures,
Mary sat at His feet in the special room.
Martha was angry with Mary for not pulling
her weight as she should for company.
But, Jesus said listening to Him
was more important than doing chores ever could be.
Spending more time with Jesus is a valuable lesson
for all of us.

Mary Magdalene of Samaria, met Jesus
at a well.
She was surprised that a Jew would talk
to a Samaritan such as herself.
Jesus asked her for a drink of water,
but said the woman would be asking
for a drink from Him if she knew
who He really was.
He could give her living water so she
would never thirst again.

Jesus told her about all the sins she
had ever done in her life.
She ran away from the well,
leaving her water pot,
and told everyone to come and see this man
she had met who knew all about her.
Jesus removed seven demons
from her that day, saving her from Hell.
Later, when Mary heard that Jesus
was at Simon's house, she went there.
She washed His feet with her tears,
dried them with her hair,
as a sign of her devotion to Him.
She also put ointment on His feet.
Jesus said she did so much for Him
because He had forgiven her of so much.
Judas Iscariot complained that this act
was a waste of ointment.
He said the oil could have been sold
and the money used for the needy to be fed.
Jesus replied that the poor would always
be with us,
but He would not always be there.
Anything done for Jesus is well worth the cost.
At the crucifixion, Mary stood at the foot
of the cross to watch her Savior bleed and die,
and later, she saw him buried in a tomb
by Joseph and Nicodemus.
Mary was the first to arrive at Jesus' tomb,
looked inside, saw linens,
but no body was inside.
Mary only saw two Angels sitting at the head
and at the foot of the rock.
The Angels said for her not to fear,
that Jesus was not here!
He arose!

Outside the tomb, Mary saw a gardener,
and asked where was Jesus' body
for her to anoint with spices and oil.
This man was no gardener; He was Jesus himself.
Jesus called her by name. She recognized
His loving, compassionate voice.
Mary was told by Jesus that she could look
upon Him, but not to touch,
as He had not gone to His Father as yet.
Mary went to tell the disciples that she
had seen the Lord! He was alive!
Mary told them to wait for Jesus in Galilee
where they later met.
Isn't it wonderful to know that Jesus loves us
in spite of what we've done.
At Calvary, Jesus paid for all our sins with the
only payment God would accept.
Only His blood can redeem us!
Be ready to answer the door of your heart
when you feel His knock.
Remember the door handle is on the inside,
only you can open it. It is your choice.

Matthew, or Levi, was a despised tax collector.
He cheated others, taking much more money
than he should.
He gave it all back when he met Jesus,
because following Jesus means
doing what Jesus would.

Matthias, along with Joseph Barsabas,
nicknamed Justus,
was nominated to replace Judas Iscariot,
who went his own selfish way.
The man chosen had to have been in the group
of followers who had been with Jesus

from His baptism by John,
then designated as a witness to His crucifixion,
then on to His ascension into Heaven.
Someone who had been there all the way.
The other disciples prayed to God
for the right choice,
knowing God knew each one inside and out.
They prayed for His will to be done
in this vital ministry,
leaving not a single doubt.
Then, in faith they drew straws.
Matthias won and became the twelfth disciple.

Mephibosheth was Jonathan's son
and King Saul's grandson.
He was five years old when his father was killed.
As a nurse was rushing to get Mephibosheth
to safety,
he was accidentally dropped, causing both feet
to become lame forever.
Later, King David asked if there was anyone
still alive in King Saul's family.
If so, he wanted to show him kindness and bestow
honor in memory of his best friend, Jonathan.
He found out that Mephibosheth, Jonathan's son,
was the only survivor.
King David sent for Mephibosheth, who was scared,
as he thought David would have him killed.
That was not the case at all,
so Mephibosheth became thrilled.
King David gave him land, and a beautiful room
where he could rest.
At King David's table, Mephibosheth was invited
to be a permanent guest.
King David treated Mephibosheth like family,
like royalty.

Methuselah was the father of Lamech
and the grandfather of Noah.
His very name means, "Longevity,"
as he lived 969 years upon this earth.
He beat Noah by 19 years, still holding
the Biblical record for his age.
His name says he was a man of the javelin,
a very strong, muscular elderly sage.
Something very old can be said to be
as old as Methuselah.
The Bible says that our days on earth can be
increased if we obey our parents from our births.
It helps too, if we can stay calm
and try not to get into a temper tantrum rage.

Micah was a Prophet in 8 BC
and a Judean countryman.
He prophesied at the same time
as Hosea and Amos in Israel.
He told what was going on
in Samaria and Jerusalem.
He was concerned about the poverty
of the farmers, pulled for the poor
against the rich,
and thought that country living
was better than city life.
Micah's goals were to rid the area of vice,
materialism, and family decay.
He preached repentance before it was too late.
He had a heart full of compassion for the lost.
He thought time was running out for the
Old Testament people of his day.
Micah was a revolutionary spokesman of Judah.

Miriam was a sister to baby Moses
and three year old Aaron.

Because the king had made a law
that all male babies were to die,
baby Moses' family had hidden him
at their home for as long as possible.
Moses had grown too big to keep
quiet at home any longer.
As Moses grew in height and weight,
so did his lungs get stronger.
To help mom, Miriam had gathered reeds
to make a basket boat for Moses.
Carefully, Miriam watched mom
water proof the little basket with pitch.
Soon, Miriam and mom put the basket bed
into the River Nile.
Both were willing to stay and quietly watch
for a little while.
They stayed until the beautiful princess
came to the water to bathe.
The princess saw the basket, and got her
servant to retrieve the little boat.
When the princess saw the cute,
round baby face, her heart got bigger.
She couldn't allow her father to destroy
this child, no never.
She would defy his law and this one boy babe,
she would save without fear.
Just at the proper time, Miriam approached
the Princess as she was looking at a wave,
asking if there was any need for a nurse?
Of course, there was a great need,
for the Princess had no clue.
She had no idea what to do.
The Princess would even pay for the nurse
to care for the baby.
Miriam found the perfect infant nurse:
Moses' real birth mom.

Moses got to stay with his real family
for about three more years.
Then, he went to live in the palace,
just as God had planned.

Mordecai, an older cousin to Esther,
was a Jewish man living in Shushan.
When Esther's parents died,
he raised her as his very own daughter.
He sent her to the Persian empire
to compete for the title of Queen
and to sit on the royal throne.
She was chosen from among many others
as King Ahasuerus's new Queen.
One day, Mordecai overheard a plot
to kill King Ahasuerus.
He sent an important message to Esther
that saved the life of her husband, the King.
When Mordecai heard about the King's advisor
named Haman who had given an order
to destroy all the Jews, he sent word to Esther.
Once again Esther was warned that she
must tell the truth about her own Jewish
heritage or else,
she and all the Jews in the 127 Jewish
states in the empire would be slaughtered.
For saving the King's life,
Mordecai was honored by the King
and given royal robes and a horse.
He rode down the roads followed
by a nobleman, Haman, of course.
Mordecai got to wear Haman's ring
that gave the royal stamp or seal
to save the Jews all over
the Persian empire,
whether in the valleys or in the hills.

Moses, a Hebrew baby, was found
in a basket at the River Nile
by Pharaoh's daughter, the Princess.
She said his own mother could nurse him
until he was weaned.
For his family it seemed only a little while.
Then, Moses must return to the palace
for a royal upbringing, the best in the land.
When Prince Moses got grown, he saw how
badly the Israelites were treated.
One day Moses killed an Egyptian guard
who was bullying one of the slaves.
After living in Egypt for forty years,
Moses ran away and escaped to Midian
in Arabia.
There, Moses stopped at a well for a drink.
As two women were getting water
for their flocks,
some rough bullies started bothering them.
He protected the two daughters of Jethro,
the Midian Priest.
Afterwards, Moses was invited to stay
at Jethro's house.
The former Prince became a shepherd
to Jethro's flocks.
Later on, Moses fell in love and married
Jethro's daughter, Zipporah.
Soon, Moses moved the flocks to Mount Horeb.
Here, God appeared to Moses in a burning bush.
However, the bush never burned up, nor did it even wilt.
God spoke from the bush and told Moses to take off
his sandals for he was standing on Holy ground.
God said He was the God of all of Moses' ancestors:
Abraham, Isaac, and Jacob.
God said that He had seen His people suffering
long enough in Egypt.

Moses was directed to go and tell Pharaoh,
"Let My people go!"
Moses started making excuses:
"Who will I say sent me?"
"I'm not a very good speaker."
"What if the Israelites won't believe me?"
God gave His responses promptly for each of these:
The "I Am" would send Moses to Egypt and to Pharaoh.
God said Moses' brother, Aaron, could do the speaking.
To conquer any doubts, God would allow Moses to throw
down his shepherd's staff which would turn into a serpent
and then turn into a staff once again.
God told Moses He would do many more signs
and wonders to show His mighty miraculous power.
Moses and Aaron then went to Goshen to meet
with the leaders of Israel who wholeheartedly believed.
God had heard His people's crying pleas.
They all bowed down and worshipped
their omnipotent God!
Through all this, God was working out His plan
to deliver the enslaved Israelites
from the Pharaoh's captive hand.
God may use you to help someone who is being bullied.

N

Naaman was a commander in chief,
or general, under King Aram.
Unfortunately, Naaman suffered
with a terrible skin disease called leprosy.
Naaman's wife had a little maid
who had been captured by King Aram.
This girl wished that Captain Naaman
could go see the Prophet Elisha of Samaria.
She believed Naaman would be healed.
His skin would look so much better.
Naaman asked King Aram if he could go
and was given permission and a letter.
Naaman carried gold, silver, clothes,
and the letter to Israel's king.
When Israel's king got the letter,
he was upset enough to rip his royal robe.
He thought this was some sort of a trick.
Soon, Elisha heard about this mix up
and sent a servant, asking Naaman to come.
When Naaman arrived at Elisha's door,
the servant told Naaman to dip
in the Jordan River exactly 7 times, no more.
Then his skin would be as good as new.
Naaman was terribly upset that Elisha

didn't come to the door himself,
but sent his servant, Gehazi.
Naaman complained that the rivers
back home were cleaner than the Jordan River.
Naaman's own servants pleaded with him
to do this one simple task.
Finally, Naaman did as he was told,
dipping himself 7 times.
Immediately, Naaman's skin was like
a new born babe's!
Naaman declared that Israel's God
was the only one on Earth.
Naaman wanted to offer a gift to Elisha,
but it was refused.
Naaman went back home like a man
who had shed both his diseased skin
and sin sick heart for new outer skin
and a new heart for God.
In the Bible, seven is a number of completion.
Had Naaman stopped dipping at number 6,
he wouldn't have been made wholly clean.
Captain Naaman returned to his home
wearing his new skin and sharing his good news.
It has been said that a little child shall lead them.
Could that little child be YOU?

Naboth owned a vineyard adjoining the land
of King Ahab.
The vineyard had been in Naboth's family
for many generations.
When Ahab wanted to buy it, Naboth would not
sale it at any price.
Tired of Ahab's pouting and wailing on his bed,
Ahab's wife, Jezebel, made a deceitful plan
in her head.
She had Naboth falsely charged of crimes

he didn't commit.
Naboth was found guilty and was stoned to death.
Then Ahab took over Naboth's property rights.
Soon after, God sent the Prophet Elijah
to visit King Ahab.
Ahab asked if Elijah was there to find him
as an enemy in God's sight.
Ahab was told that dogs would drink his blood, too,
where they had drunk Naboth's blood when he died.
Don't covet what belongs to your neighbor.
You'll be in danger of losing God's favor.

Nahum was a Prophet in Israel in 7 BC.
He preached against the enemy of Assyria
and its capital city of Nineveh.
He proclaimed that God would judge
the enemy as well as their own country, Israel.
He urged the people to take their eyes
off the Assyrians, their worst enemy.
Nahum urged them to focus only on their
inward selves.
They should pray to the sovereign God
in the quietness of their souls.
The noise of their enemy distracted them
from focusing on the conditions of their hearts.
Life is full of choices. Set priorities and make time
for the most important part.
Do we let outside interferences rob us
of our quiet time with God?
We can pray inside our closets, down on our knees,
or while lifting up our hands and face.
We can pray about anything at anytime at any place.

Naomi was the mother-in-law of Ruth.
Both widowed, the two of them became a family.
Working, sharing, helping each other along the way,
as all God's people should do everyday, anyway.

Nathan was a prophet and a leading figure
in King David's court.
In the contest between David's sons,
Adonijah and Solomon, for the throne,
Nathan sided with Solomon, thinking Adonijah
would be totally wrong.
Along with Zadok, the Priest, Nathan anointed
Solomon as the new King.
God had earlier proclaimed that Solomon
would build the temple in Jerusalem.
Nothing or no one would get in the way
of Solomon's wearing of David's royal ring.

Nehemiah, a Jewish man, lived in the days of Ezra.
His job was to serve wine to the king.
He loved the city of Jerusalem, asking
about it when any visitors came from there.
It was reported that the people were so poor
and not respected in the least.
Jerusalem's walls were broken down
and her gates were burned.
Piles of rubbish and trash lay in heaps.
This sad news caused Nehemiah to weep
because he was so concerned.
He cried out to God to hear his prayers
of anguish for his beloved city.
When he again served the King,
it was evident that Nehemiah was sad.
When asked about it, Nehemiah said
the city of Jerusalem lay in ruins.
The King asked how he could help.
What could he do to show his pity?
Nehemiah's solution was that he
be granted permission to go and rebuild
the city of Jerusalem where God
promised to gather His people one day.

Nehemiah's wish was granted gladly
by the King, and he eagerly made haste.
He and a group of horsemen rode
for one thousand miles
to Jerusalem, a very long way.
He told no one about God's plan
for three whole days.
At night, he and a few men checked
out the walls and the gates,
seeing much rubble.
Nehemiah saw his beloved city
lying in useless waste.
Gathering men around, he told
what God had done in his life.
How the King had sent him there,
so that God's people would be respected.
The people were moved to join in the work,
ready to get started right away!
Soon, the locals began mocking them,
asking if they were rebelling
against the King, trying to cause trouble?
Their answer was that the God of Heaven
would give His servants success.
No outside help was needed.
No others could share in this work.
Each family built a part of the wall,
a high Priest built a gate,
and a rich man built a long section
of the wall.
Some contributed a lot to the project.
Some, very little; Some, nothing at all.
After fifty-two days, the wall was completed,
with gates closed, and guards posted.
Their enemies were afraid, knowing God
had helped these Jews
build this wall to protect His people.

Nimrod was the son of Cush
and the grandson of Ham, by birth.
Genesis says he was a mighty hunter
before the Lord.
Also, it says he was the first great
warrior on Earth.
His kingdom got its start with Babel,
then it spread beyond.
Vast tracts of land in Mesopotamia
were ruled by Nimrod.

Noah, his wife, his three sons,
and all their wives,
were laughed at and made fun of
for 120 years.
Even though it had never rained,
God said to build a three story ark.
God said He would destroy all the people
on the Earth.
He was even sorry for their births.
Noah was to gather two of every kind
of animal, some would have seven.
Only his own family would be spared
from the coming flood.
Noah told everyone who wasn't on the boat
would drown in the water, or else
get trampled, and suffocate in the mud.
At the right time, God said to enter the boat.
God closed the door.
It rained for forty days and forty nights,
not one drop more.
Afterwards, Noah sent out a dove
on three different days.
The first time, the dove came back very quickly.
The second time, the dove brought back an olive leaf.
This was a sign the Earth was drying out.

The third time, the dove never returned to the boat.
After a year, Noah and his family
finally got off the ark.
The first thing Noah did was to make an altar
and looked toward Heaven above.
Noah wanted to give thanks for their safety.
Noah offered gifts to God and then,
God made a promise to Noah.
God would put a rainbow in the sky
as a promise to him and to all of us.
He would never again destroy
the whole earth with a flood.
The four seasons would come and go.
Noah was to rule the world and
God wanted Noah's family to grow.
There are over 7,000 promises
in our Bible. God has kept everyone!
You can rely on this number one belief.

O

Obadiah was a Prophet and a writer
of the Old Testament's shortest book.
Obadiah was sent from God to deliver
a message to the people of Edom.
These descendants of Esau were known
as the Edomites.
Esau's brother, Jacob, was the father
of Israel, its people, the Israelites.
The two nations had been fighting
for years in wars and rivalry.
When Israel was taken into exile
by the Assyrians, then the Babylonians,
Edom did absolutely nothing
as her relatives got beat up,
ending in much misery.
Obadiah said that Edom should not
have stood by with a delighted look.
Obadiah said Edom was the villain
and Israel was the victim in this episode.
Obadiah warned that God would allow
what was done to Israel
to be done to Edom.
There is an old saying
that you reap what you sow.

Obadiah was a Governor in the house of King Ahab.
He feared God and had been very devout
since he was small.
Once, he hid one hundred Prophets of God
in two caves to save them from the persecution
of Queen Jezebel.
Obadiah supplied them with food and water
freely-keeping no tab.
Later, King Ahab ordered Obadiah to find water
during a dry spell.
Obadiah went one way; Ahab went another way.
Obadiah suddenly saw Elijah, and bowed down
in reverence to him, kneeling in awe.
Elijah told Obadiah to return to King Ahab
and say he had found Elijah.
Obadiah was afraid that he would be killed
by King Ahab, for naught.
For years, King Ahab had searched for Elijah,
but to no avail.
Now, Obadiah didn't want any attention
drawn to him, risking his all.
But, Elijah said he would meet King Ahab face
to face that very day.
Obadiah went to the King with Elijah's message,
and the two men met.
Obadiah did the hard thing, but the right thing.
Don't be slack and just take the easy way out.

One thief on the cross, the Bible doesn't tell
us his name,
hung beside Jesus and watched as Jesus
showed forgiveness to all those
who hurt Him, to all who caused Him pain.
Yet, Jesus was merciful to those
who did not understand
why He came to earth to save
every, repentant, sinful man.

The thief knew he had done wrong.
He knew he deserved to die.
He believed Jesus was the perfect Lamb
of God who took our sins upon Him.
The thief asked for Jesus to remember him
when He came into His kingdom that day.
Jesus answered that this thief
would certainly join Him in Paradise
that very day!
This joyful man died knowing
such a comforting spirit of relief.
You can't go to Heaven by being good.
God says our best is like filthy rags.
You can't depend on what others
in your family have done,
or by minding your manners,
or by acting very nice.
You must be born again.
You must be saved by Jesus' blood.
Your name must be written
in the Lamb's Book of Life.

Onesimus was a runaway slave
owned by Philemon.
He was met, befriended, and converted
under Paul's teachings.
Paul wrote an Epistle to Philemon
recorded in the New Testament.
Onesimus traveled back to his owner,
carrying his own mail.
The letter requested that Philemon
forgive, set free, and return
Onesimus back to Paul, as he
had been of great help to him while in jail.
Paul referred to Onesimus
as a Christian brother, certainly, one of us.
Paul saw missionary material in Onesimus.

P

Paul was changed from a persecutor
of the Jews to a believer in Jesus
when his physical eyes were blinded
by an awesome, bright light.
And now as a new creature in Christ,
he's no longer called Saul, but Paul.
After that Damascus Road experience,
Paul gained an innermost, spiritual sight.

Peter, first a fisher of fish,
later, a fisher of men,
followed Jesus, then denied Him
three times before the rooster crowed.
He realized that Jesus had been right
all along as He had foretold.
Jesus had asked Peter three times
if he loved Him.
Peter was adamant that there was
no doubt about his allegiance.
Peter was ashamed, felt sorry, and cried
on his knees over his sin.
Jesus forgave him and later at Pentecost,
Peter preached.
There 3,000 souls for Jesus were reached.

We can help catch the fish,
but Jesus is the only One
Who is able to clean them.

Philemon received the letter from Paul
about Onesimus' new faith.
Philemon, an Epistle in the New Testament,
is only one chapter in length.
Philemon was an authority figure
in the Christian churches in Asia Minor.

Philip was told by an angel of God
to walk over to the road
that goes from Jerusalem down to Gaza
at noon one day.
He did so, and there met an Ethiopian eunuch
coming down the road from Jerusalem,
where he had been on a pilgrimage.
The eunuch was riding in the Queen
of Ethiopia's chariot.
The eunuch was the minister in charge
of finances for Queen Candace.
As he was riding along, he was reading
the Prophet Isaiah's words.
The Spirit of God told Philip to climb
into the eunuch's chariot.
Philip had to run along in haste
beside the chariot until he
could safely hop aboard.
Philip asked if the eunuch understood
what he was reading?
Was there any explanation he required?
The reply was that the eunuch needed
some help with this passage, indeed.
Philip took this opportunity to explain
about Jesus to the eunuch on their way.

As they traveled on, they came to a stream
of water, deep enough to cover the waist.
The eunuch asked why he could
not be baptized there.
The chariot stopped, and both men
went down to the water.
Philip baptized the eunuch on the spot,
not waiting any longer.
As both men came up out of the water,
the Holy Spirit immediately whisked Phillip
up and away from the eunuch's view.
The eunuch never saw Philip again.
But he was so happy! He had his reward.
He had what he came for and went on down
the road toward home, feeling clean and new.

Priscilla was the wife of Aquilla.
Both were makers of tents.
She was a great helper to her husband
in all wifely ways.
Priscilla could help Aquilla make a tent,
do the baking,
and then, wash all the dishes.
They befriended Paul on his journeys
by hosting him at their home.
Priscilla never charged Paul
a penny of rent.
She told Paul to feel free to come
and goas he saw fit,
whatever were his wishes.
Priscilla was a true friend to Paul
and a godly wife to Aquilla.

Prodigal Son, his brother, and their father
were nameless men in a parable
that Jesus told long ago.

The younger son wanted his inheritance
early so he could go to see the world.
Hesitantly, the father agreed,
and gave him his fortune,
his share of the money.
This son squandered all his money
away in a very short time.
Soon, he was in rags, and got a job
feeding slop to some nasty smelling pigs.
He was starving; No one even offered him
any corn cobs to eat.
One day, this son realized he would
be better off if he returned to the family fold.
Even his father's hired servants
ate three meals a day, at least.
The son decided to go home,
repent to God and to his father.
He was even willing to ask for a job
as a hired hand.
As he neared home, his father
saw him coming and rejoiced!
He ran out, hugged and kissed his son.
His eyes were very moist.
The son was trying to ask for both
his father's and God's forgiveness.
But, his father never heard him at all.
Instead, the father was giving orders
for a clean set of digs,
a ring for his finger, a pair of sandals
for his feet,
and a menu for a feast of barbecued beef.
Meanwhile, the older son
came in from the fields,
and heard the joyful sounds.
He was told about his brother's return
to the family's land.
He grew angry and refused to join

the celebration of the family reunion.
The father tried to reason with him,
but he wouldn't listen with his heart.
He listened with his mind, and asked why
he never had a party.
He had stayed home, working the fields,
never causing his father any grief.
The father's answer was that everything
he owned belonged to this elder son,
who had always been with him.
The feast was for the son they thought
was dead,
but who now was very much alive.
It was for the son who was lost
and now has been found.

Publius was a leader on the part
of the island of Malta where Paul
and others landed after being ship-
wrecked on their way to Rome.
Publius took everyone into his home
as his guests.
He dried them out, and hosted them
for the next three days,
allowing them to get much needed rest.
Publius' father was there, too,
but was sick with a high fever.
Paul went to the old man's room,
laid hand on him, and earnestly prayed.
Instantly, Publius' father was healed.
Word spread around the island and many
sick people came to see Paul.
God's answer to Paul's prayer resulted
in increasing the number of believers
and encouraging all who were depressed.
Publius was a man of great hospitality.
He had a caring, tender, and loving heart.

R

Rahab was a woman who lived in Canaan.
She hid Caleb and Joshua on the roof
of her house and lied to their enemies
at the door down below.
For her help, she asked that she
and all her family be saved
when the city was attacked.
They promised not to harm her
or her family if she would do her part.
She was to lower a red cord out her
window to show a believing heart.
Rahab was spared by the cord of "red,"
just as the Israelites were passed over
by the "Death Angel" who saw
the lamb's blood over their door posts.
This spiritual color of "red" stands
for the shed blood of Jesus that saves
us and washes us "white" as snow.

Rebecca, a beautiful young shepherdess,
came to the well to get water for her sheep.
And because she was so thoughtful and kind,
she offered a drink to Eliezer,
and also to the rest.

Not knowing these were the clues
needed to select Isaac's new wife,
Rebecca clearly showed that she
was the only one suitable to wear
Isaac's bride's dress.

Rechab was a teetotaler, who ordered
his son, Jonadab, and his future grandsons
to never drink wine,
not even one drop.
Even when the Prophet Jeremiah
offered them wine, they abstained.
They refused, saying that their ancestors
commanded this bold stand.
And down through the ages, they had all
followed through with this plan.
Jeremiah told the Recabites what
God-of-the-Angel-Armies had assured.
The God of Israel promised that,
"There will always be a descendant
of Jonadab, son of Rechab,
at My service! Always!"
What a disciplined life
for this family clan!

Ruth, a recent widow, chose to stay
with Naomi, her mother in law.
Instead of going back to her own family,
Ruth said she'd go where Naomi would go,
said Naomi's people would be her people,
and Naomi's God would be her God.
That's a very good example of true loyalty.

S

Salome was the wife of Zebedee,
and the mother of James and John.
She was a friend, or possible sister,
to Mary, the mother of Jesus.
Once she asked Jesus if her boys
could have special seats in Heaven.
Salome was one of the women at the foot
of the cross at the crucifixion,
and later carried spices to the tomb
to anoint Jesus' body.
Salome and the other women
found the tomb empty!
They were told to tell the disciples
to go to Galilee
and wait there for Jesus.

Samson was to never to shave his hair,
or else, his Nazarite vow would be broken.
And God would leave him and he'd lose
all of his strength.
Delilah found out the secret of his strength
by tricking Samson.
She received 1,100 pieces of silver for her deceit.
Samson was taken as a prisoner.

His eyes were gouged out.
His enemies didn't notice his hair's new growth.
Maybe they didn't even care.
Soon blinded Samson was able to pull down
the columns of Dagon's temple
while he sat near there.
He killed 3,000 Philistines without even using
one eye, much less both.

Samuel was the promised son
of Hannah and Elkanah.
He was to be taken to the temple
to work with Eli, the Priest.
One night, while at the temple,
Samuel heard a voice calling his name.
He got up and went to Eli, but Eli
had not called him in the least.
After the third time this occurred,
Priest Eli knew it must be God's voice
calling out to Samuel. Eli told Samuel
that he really had no choice,
but to answer His Lord, and be willing
to trust God first and obey His command.
Then retell all of it to Eli, the Priest.

Shadrach, Meshach, and Abednego
were Daniel's three Hebrew friends.
They refused to worship the ninety foot
golden statue that King Nebuchadnezzar
had ordered the people to do or else,
be thrown into a fiery furnace.
The fire was made seven times hotter
for Daniel's friends to burn.
The guards who threw them in were killed
by the blazing flames at the door.
Daniel's friends were not burned,

nor did they even smell like smoke.
The king said three men had been put
into the fire, but now there were four.
Surely, they were joined by God's Son!
In serving God, they were so earnest!

Shunammite lady and her husband
were helpful to Elisha, the Prophet.
She invited Elisha home for a meal
one time, and after that, it became
his habit to stop and share a meal
when he passed their way.
The lady told her husband that Elisha
was surely a holy man.
They decided to build on an extra room
upstairs for him to stay.
In Elisha's room, they added a chair,
a desk, a lamp, and a comfortable bed.
Elisha was very thankful and asked
through his servant, Gehazi,
if there was anything they could ask
for her from the King or the army commander.
The lady said she had all she needed;
She was secure with her family.
Elisha wasn't satisfied with her answer.
Gehazi noticed she had no child.
The lady was called in and told
that next year, she would have a son.
The boy was born just as
Elisha had foretold
and he grew bigger every day.
Later, he ran to his father,
complaining of a terrible pain in his head.
A servant carried him to his mother's lap
where he lay until noon
when he died in her arms, breaking her heart.

She carried they boy up to Elisha's bed,
lay him down, and then left him.
She told her husband to get
a servant and a donkey,
so she could go see the holy man, Elisha.
She failed to say their son was dead.
As she got closer to Mount Carmel,
Elisha could see her,
and sent Gehazi to ask what was the matter?
Why was she in such a race?
The lady said everything's fine,
but when she got to Elisha, she fell apart.
Elisha ordered Gehazi to go fast,
not to speak to anyone,
and lay his staff across the boy's face.
Nothing happened, still no sign of life
appeared on Elisha's bed.
When Elisha arrived, he went to his room,
locked the door, and prayed.
He then stretched out fully upon the boy:
(mouth on mouth, eyes on eyes,
arms on arms, legs on legs).
The body soon felt warm to the touch.
Elisha got up, paced the room,
then stretched out over the boy a second time.
Amazingly, the boy sneezed seven times
and then opened his eyes wide.
Elisha called Gehazi to get the lady
in to see and hug her son,
whom was loved very much.
The Shunammite lady fell in awe
at Elisha's feet, facedown in humility,
then hugged her son with a mother's touch,
as God had healed her son in Shunem that day.

Silas was chosen, along with Judas,
to go with Paul and Barnabas

to the church in Antioch.
Silas and Judas held considerable
weight in the church.
They were trusted by the members,
who knew them well.
They were to carry a letter with some
guidelines to keep the peace between
Jews and non-Jews,
concerning religious practices.
The main points of the letter
said for Christians to be sure
to avoid idols, never eat offensive foods,
and guard the values of sex and marriage.
Also, don't get hung up on the rites
of circumcision; It's not worth a lot.
After arriving at the Antioch church,
Silas and Judas read the letter.
Silas and Judas were both good preachers,
sharing words of encouragement, and hope,
making everyone feel much better.
They both were accepted by the church
wholeheartedly that day.
Later on, Paul chose Silas to go
with him to Syria and Cilicia
to build up the congregations there,
and to others as they traveled along the way.

Shepherds, watching their sheep
on the hillside at night
were suddenly startled
by a very bright light.
They were the very first humans
to hear the news of Jesus' birth.
As angels told them not to fear
then sang praises to God for His Son
had been born in Bethlehem that day.
The shepherds were told to follow the star

and travel along that way to Bethlehem.
After seeing the baby Jesus,
the shepherds shared the good news
of the Savior's birth so all could hear.
Lowly shepherds, not men of wealth nor fame,
were highly honored to behold this Holy scene.
Dirty smelly shepherds were invited first
to view the newborn King.

Simeon, an old man, was told by the Spirit
to come to the temple that day.
According to the law, Jesus' parents
were coming, too, for His dedication.
Simeon got to hold the baby in his arms
and offer praises to God above,
for extending his days, to be able
to show his love in celebration,
for allowing him to live long enough
to see the people's Salvation.
"He'll light the way for all the Gentiles
to see God," Simeon proclaimed.
"And He's the glory of your people Israel,"
Simeon furthermore exclaimed.
Simeon said he could now leave this life
in peace, after seeing Jesus face to face
and eye to eye.
Simeon was now ready for his home on high.

Simon the Leper opened his home
in Bethany for Jesus to be his guest.
While eating dinner there, a woman
came to Jesus and poured expensive
perfume on His head,
rolling down His body to His feet,
then flowing onto the floor.
The disciples were furious about such

a waste of such a possible revenue.
They thought the perfume could have been sold,
their expenses met, and still have money
to spend on the poor with the rest.
Jesus said that she was doing this anointing
to His body as an act for burial.
Jesus said there would always be the poor
among us, but, He would not be here always,
as He had told them often enough before.
Jesus said she did what she could
when she could; Her timing was perfect.
Jesus foretold that whenever His Message
was preached around the world,
this woman's gesture would be remembered
with admiration by me and you.

Simon of Cyrene was the father
of Rufus and Alexander.
As Simon was coming in from the countryside
on his way home from work,
the Roman soldiers grabbed him by the arm
and turned him around with a powerful jerk.
Simon was ordered to pick up Jesus' cross,
as Jesus was too weak
from His cruel treatment,
which was considerably abusive, more than just mean.
Simon had to walk behind Jesus and carry His cross
up to Golgotha's Hill.
Unknowingly, to the Romans, Simon's disobedience
to their commander
turned out to be an act of honor of will
and a privilege for Simon of Cyrene.

Solomon was the second son
of King David and Bathsheba.
At his birth, the Prophet Nathan

named him Jeddah,
which means, "Loved by God."
God told David that at his death,
Solomon would become king
because he was a man of peace, not war.
At the alter at Gibeon, Solomon offered
a thousand sacrifices to God.
When asked what Solomon wanted from God,
he answered, "Wisdom and knowledge to know
right and wrong, how to rule the people."
God was pleased with this unselfish request
for within his heart God saw the real man.
Solomon could have asked for a long life,
riches, power, or victory.
God said Solomon would be granted more
wisdom than anyone forever.
Once, Solomon made a wise decision
concerning a baby's true mother.
He knew the lady willing to spare the baby's life
from the deadly sword
was the true mother who genuinely
loved the baby more.
All of Israel was amazed at Solomon's wisdom!
They stood in awe!
Also, God would add all the other choices
he could've had as a bonus, after all.
As a reward, King Solomon would be
allowed to rebuild the temple.
Building God's temple was Solomon's
most important work of all!
The Ark of the Covenant was placed
inside the temple's Holy of Holies.
It took seven years to complete
this project with utmost care.
Afterwards, Solomon and the people
worshipped their Holy God there.

One night, God visited Solomon at the temple,
and said therein He would dwell and bless it
as long as Solomon followed Him.
At the bottom of the temple
was Solomon's magnificent palace.
With so many pillars of cedar around it,
it looked like a forest, indeed.
Some called it, "The House of the Forest
of Lebanon."
From this place, Solomon walked up
the staircase made of stone
to enter the temple more easily.
Sometimes, the Queen of Sheba came
to visit him, bringing him treasures.
After asking him questions, and hearing
his wisdom, she said, "God has blessed."
King Solomon ruled in Israel for forty years,
then went to his rest.
Many of his wise sayings are recorded
in our Bible in the book of Proverbs.

Stephen was the first Christian martyr.
About his beliefs, he would never barter.
Saul was the one who ordered Stephen
stoned to death.
Saul watched in the background,
while men stood around
in a circle picking up heavy, jagged stones.
They threw them hard with all their might,
thus, breaking his very bones.
Stephen continued to look toward heaven,
praying until his dying breath.

T

Tabitha, also called Gazelle,
and Dorcas in Greek, was a disciple
in Joppa, known for her goodness
and her willingness to help others.
During the time that Peter was in Lydda,
she became sick and died.
Tabitha's friends prepared her body
for burial and put it in a cool room.
Some other disciples sent for Peter
to come to Joppa to Tabitha's house.
Peter arrived and was taken to the room
where Tabitha's body was laid.
Inside, there were many women
showing off the clothes made by Tabitha.
They shared her gift of sewing.
Happily, they cried.
They meant well.
Urgently, Peter asked the women to leave,
and he knelt at the body to pray.
Peter, then spoke directly to the body,
"Tabitha, get up today."
At once, Tabitha opened her eyes,
saw Peter and sat up on the bed.
Peter took her hand and helped her

to get up even faster.
Next, Peter called the believers
and the women and presented a living
Tabitha from head to toe or toe to head.
As this miracle spread around Joppa,
many came to trust in the Master.

Theophilus was an honorable man to whom
two books, (Luke and Acts), were written
by Luke, and found in the New Testament.
The first volume, Luke, tells the story
of Jesus from the beginning
to His Ascension into Heaven above.
The second volume, Acts, continues the story
of Jesus, but expands to challenge us to live
out our lives in genuine Christian action.
Daily serving Him is the best witness to others,
as shown by the Apostles.
No act, whether great or small,
goes unnoticed by the Father of Love!
Each will represent our gratitude to God
for His eternal investment.

Thomas, the Doubter, had to see
for himself before he could believe.
He questioned Jesus whether His nail
prints were really real.
Jesus offered to allow Thomas
to put his finger into his wounded
scarred hands and feel.
Afterwards, Thomas's doubts
were no more.
By feeling, those doubts
were forever transformed.
The Bible says those who believe

by faith, without seeing, to receive
salvation are truly blessed.

Timothy, as a lad, learned scriptures
at mother Eunice's knee.
As a teen, he served as a missionary
with Silas, Luke, and Paul.
He traveled all around the cities
of Galilee, telling the gospel story
he had heard all his growing up years.
Imitating his mentors and without hesitation,
Timothy knew God would conquer any fears.
Therefore, Timothy had no reservations.
Timothy answered God's call.

Titus was a Gentile of Antioch,
who was taken by Paul
to a conference in Jerusalem in AD 48.
The main issue argued at this meeting
was essentially about whether or not
uncircumcised non-Jews could be admitted
to the Christian community.
There was a much heated debate.
This conflict would long be remembered.
Titus was not circumcised by Paul,
as Paul refused to have any part.
Paul wanted the Faith to belong to all men,
Gentile or Jew,
based solely on the beliefs in their hearts.
Titus became Paul's symbol of his strong belief
in this issue of Christian equality.
Titus traveled with Paul on his second journey.
Titus later became an important member
of Paul's staff, serving as a fellow missionary.

W

Warriors for Christ, we have a mission
to fight in a battle between good and evil.
We need the proper training and the armor of God:
(A belt of truth, a shield of faith, a helmet
of salvation, a breastplate of righteousness,
a sword of the Spirit, and gospel shoes).
We prayerfully follow our orders of His commission
to go into all the world, telling the Good News.

Whosoever, that means anyone at all.
Young and old, strong and weak, big and small
can follow Jesus, just answer His call.
It is easy as ABC-123.
Admit, Believe, and Confess.
Thereafter, your life, He will surely bless.

Wise men, three in all, studied the night time
skies, looking at the stars.
When they saw a special star in the east,
they followed it from afar
to Jerusalem with just one question in mind.
Where is the King of the Jews born?
We want to honor Him.
King Herod found out, asked his chief priests

and scribes, no doubt,
where the Christ would be born?
King Herod's men knew their history.
The Prophet Micah had foretold
that the ruler of Israel would be born
in Bethlehem hundreds of years ago.
Herod told the wise men to let him know,
so he could also worship Him.
The three wise men bearing gifts of gold,
myrrh, and frankincense,
arrived at the home of Jesus when He
was about two years old.
They humbly bowed down to Him
in Godly reverence.
One wise man had a dream not to return
and tell King Herod the child's location,
for surely it was a trap.
They were told to travel home a different route.
Another road would be a much safer way
on the Egyptian map.

Ye, all of mankind on planet Earth,
This includes men and women, girls and boys,
babies, teenagers, and senior adults,
and even fetuses waiting on their delivery.
All were created in God's own image.
He has loved you with an everlasting love.
He has known your name before your birth.
And He has a special plan for you
now throughout eternity.

Z

Zacchaeus was a wee little man.
He was very curious about Jesus.
While standing on the ground
where he couldn't see,
he had the idea to climb
up a nearby sycamore tree.
Jesus pointed up and said to him,
"Zacchaeus, you come down,
for I'm going to your house today."
The crowds were amazed that Jesus
would even speak to, never converse,
much less go to a house of a sinner
and maybe with him, eat a little dinner.
After their visit, Zacchaeus
wanted to give half of his money
to the poor and repay four times
as much as he had cheated
to each citizen in the province.
Jesus totally changed Zacchaeus
on the inside of his heart first.
Then his outside actions could help
his neighbors, more easily be convinced.
When Jesus makes a house call,
He surely knows your number.

So be sure to be ready and awake,
never dozing or be in a slumber.

Zacharias was a Priest in the Holy
Place in the Temple.
He was the husband of Elizabeth,
the Virgin Mary's cousin.
One day, the angel Gabriel
brought him some very good news.
When told he and his wife, Elizabeth,
would have a child in their old age,
Zechariah didn't believe that this
announcement could possibly be true.
As a sign, God kept him from talking
until the birth of his son.
As a Priest, communicating wasn't simple.
When he named his boy, John,
his tongue was finally set free
from its warm, moist physical cage.
This miracle kept the town talk a' buzzing.

Zadok was a Priest who helped
the Prophet Nathan
to secure Solomon's place
on King David's throne
upon David's death.
Zadok was rewarded for his effort
by being named the Chief Priest.
Zadok the Priest and Nathan the Prophet
anointed Solomon as the new King.
Working together makes for a stronger bond.
Two cords stranded in unison are harder to undo.

Zebedee was the husband of Salome
and the father of James and John.
Zebedee's wife tried to get her sons

into special seats when they got to Heaven.
Zebedee's wife was rebuked soundly
by Jesus for her selfish request.
All seats in Heaven will be front row,
center aisle at no charge to you and me.
It cost Jesus His life but, He gave it willingly.
Jesus paid the cost with His blood at Calvary.

Zechariah was a prophet in late 6 BC.
He and Haggai the Prophet worked together
to encourage the people of Judah to rebuild
the ruined temple quickly.
Zechariah knew his people had also lost touch
with who they were in God's sight, too.
They had lost their identity.
He preached to them energetic messages
and shared his visions of God's sovereignty.
Zechariah's words are still relevant today
as our world has little regard
for the things of God and His purpose
for our mortal beings.

Zephaniah was a Prophet and probably
a great grandson of King Hezekiah.
He was an educated man who lived in 7 BC.
He preached to the ruling class of Judah,
as well as, to the enemies of Judah,
the Philistines, and the Assyrians
about God's wrath to come.
On the other hand, Zephaniah,
like Amos, believed that God
always would have a remnant of believers
who would carry on the throne of David.
Can you be counted on to be part
of something bigger than what you can see?

Acknowledgements

Praises to our Lord and Savior, Jesus Christ, who inspired the ideals of this book. Many thanks to the following people for their invaluable contributions:

- My husband, Derrell Shaw, who exemplifies being a Christian husband and father.

- My two daughters, Anna and Amy, who believed I could do this book, and who are raising my grandchildren in their Christian homes.

- Mr. Michael Bearden and Dr. Condy Richardson, who took time away from their busy schedules to write the forewords, after checking on my theology.

- Much gratitude goes to my close friends, Sarah Massey, Jeannie Peed, and June Roper for encouraging and praying me through this writing experience.

May God richly bless each of you!

All proceeds from this book will help fund:

CONNIE MAXWELL CHILDREN"S HOME
PO Box 118
Greenwood, SC
29648-1178
www.ConnieMaxwell.com

Printed in the United States
By Bookmasters